MW01118043

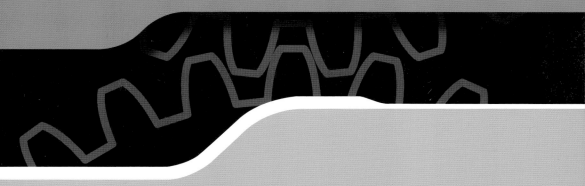

Technology Through the Ages
Prehistory and the
Classical Period

BROWN
BEAR
BOOKS

Published by Brown Bear Books Limited

An imprint of:
The Brown Reference Group Ltd
68 Topstone Road
Redding
Connecticut 06896
USA
www.brownreference.com

© 2009 The Brown Reference Group Ltd

ISBN: 978-1-933834-83-2

Editorial Director: Lindsey Lowe
Managing Editor: Tim Harris
Project Director: Graham Bateman
Editors: Briony Ryles, Derek Hall
Designer: Steve McCurdy
Picture Research: Steve McCurdy

Library of Congress Cataloging-in-Publication Data available upon request

Picture Credits

Cover image
Segovia aqueduct, Spain (Shutterstock, Carolina)

Shutterstock:
19 Ints Vikmanis; 35 zhuda; 37 WitR; 43 Jeff Schultes; 47 Maugli; 51 PhotoJimy; 53 Hannah Gleghorn; 54–55 Vladislav Gurfinkel; 59 Styve Reineck; 63 Joakim Lloyd Raboff; 79 YellowCrest Media; 81 WitR; 82–83 Elena Elisseeva; 85 Natalia Bratslavsky.

Photos.com:
22–23; 27; 31; 36; 67; 69; 73–74; 77; 89; 90

Artwork © The Brown Reference Group Ltd

The Brown Reference Group Ltd has made every effort to trace copyright holders of the pictures used in this book. Anyone having claims to ownership not identified above is invited to contact The Brown Reference Group Ltd.

Printed in the United States of America

Contents

Introduction

Technology through the Ages forms part of the Curriculum Connections project. This six-volume set describes the story of scientific discovery from the earliest use of fire and the development of the wheel through to space travel, modern computing, and the Human Genome Project. Each volume in the set covers a major historical period, ranging from prehistory up to modern times.

Within each volume there are two types of article:

In-Depth articles form the core of the work, and focus on scientific discoveries and technological progress of particular note, giving background to the topic, information about the people involved, and explanations of how the discoveries or inventions have been put to use. Each article focuses on a particular step forward that originated within this period, but the articles often extend back into the history of the topic or forward to later developments to help give further context to each subject. Boxed features add to the information, often explaining scientific principles.

Within each article there are two key aids to learning, which are to be found in color bars located in the margins of each page:

Curriculum Context sidebars indicate to the reader that a subject has particular relevance to certain key State and National Science and Technology Education Standards up to Grade 12.

Glossary sidebars define key words within the text.

Timeline Articles, to be found at the end of each volume, list year-by-year scientific discoveries, inventions, technological advances, and key dates of exploration. For each period, the Timelines are divided into horizontal bands that each focus on a particular theme of technology or science.

A summary *Glossary* lists the key terms defined in the volume, and the *Index* lists people and major topics covered. Fully captioned *Illustrations* play a major role in the set, and include early prints and paintings, contemporary photographs, artwork reconstructions, and explanatory diagrams.

About this Volume

In this volume (*Prehistory and the Classical Period— prehistory to 0 A.D.*), we cover the period from the emergence of modern humans to the birth of Christianity—the latter being the final years of Roman dominance in the Mediterranean region.

The history of science dates back to the history of humankind itself. Early people shaped stone pebbles into tools, and they used the tools to fashion weapons and other artifacts from bone, antler, and wood. Significantly, they also learned how to use fire. The next major step came with the cultivation of plants for food (particularly cereals), and the use of animals for food, wool, hides, and as draft creatures. This period led to the 'urbanization' of many societies, with large cities and communities appearing.

Recorded history began with the invention of writing, meaning that information could be passed on, and also with the development of numbers and counting systems and of weights and measures, to enable accurate records to be made of crops harvested and traded. To keep track of the seasons, calendars were devised, and with this came a growing understanding of the night sky—marking the beginnings of astronomy, the first of the sciences to be studied.

With developing civilizations came new construction technologies, epitomized by the Egyptian and Mesoamerican pyramids, the temples of the Greeks, and the roads and aqueducts of the Romans. But major conflicts between societies also increased, and the development of ever more sophisticated weapons of war became an essential part of technological innovation and scientific research. Toward the end of the period it is possible to identify the first true scientists and philosophers, for example the mathematician, engineer, and inventor Archimedes.

Early humans

The story of human evolution began more than 5 million years ago with early hominids living in Africa. The first real humans appeared about 2.4 million years ago in East Africa. They learned to make fire and gradually became skilled in shaping tools, mainly as aids to survival but also later for ceremonial use.

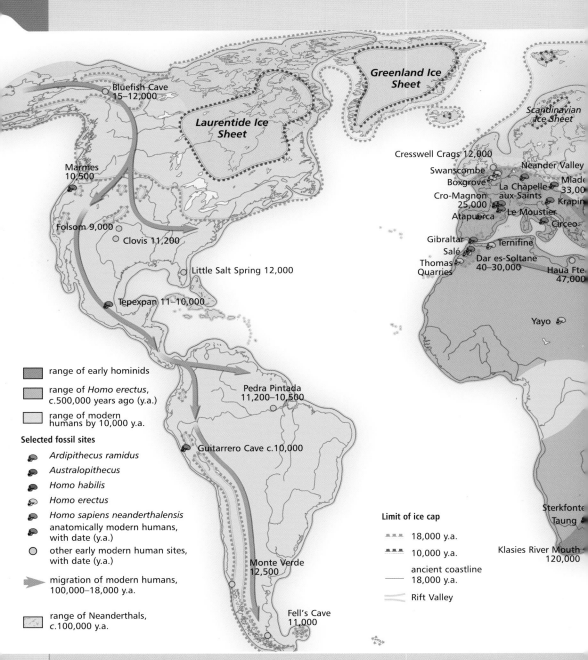

Greenland Ice Sheet

Scandinavian Ice Sheet

Bluefish Cave 15–12,000

Laurentide Ice Sheet

Cresswell Crags 12,000

Swanscombe
Boxgrove
Cro-Magnon 25,000
Atapuerca

Neander Valley
La Chapelle-aux-Saints
Le Moustier

Mlade
33,00
Krapin
Circeo

Marmes 10,500

Folsom 9,000

Clovis 11,200

Little Salt Spring 12,000

Tepexpan 11–10,000

Gibraltar
Salé
Thomas Quarries

Ternifine
Dar es-Soltane 40–30,000

Haua Fte 47,000

Yayo

Pedra Pintada 11,200–10,500

Guitarrero Cave c.10,000

range of early hominids

range of Homo erectus, c.500,000 years ago (y.a.)

range of modern humans by 10,000 y.a.

Selected fossil sites

- Ardipithecus ramidus
- Australopithecus
- Homo habilis
- Homo erectus
- Homo sapiens neanderthalensis
- anatomically modern humans, with date (y.a.)
- ○ other early modern human sites, with date (y.a.)
- migration of modern humans, 100,000–18,000 y.a.
- range of Neanderthals, c.100,000 y.a.

Limit of ice cap

- 18,000 y.a.
- 10,000 y.a.
- ancient coastline 18,000 y.a.
- Rift Valley

Sterkfonte
Taung

Klasies River Mouth 120,000

Monte Verde 12,500

Fell's Cave 11,000

The first tools

Human ancestors were making tools about 2.3 million years ago in Ethiopia and about 2.25 million years ago in China. Nearly 2 million years ago at Olduvai Gorge, Tanzania, "handy man" (*Homo habilis*) was making choppers by striking one stone against another. Choppers were used for cutting or sawing, and the

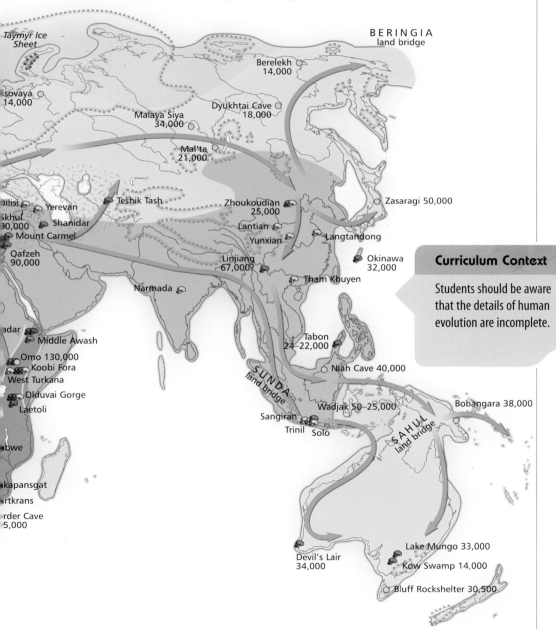

BERINGIA
land bridge

Taymyr Ice
Sheet

Berelekh
14,000

isovaya
14,000

Dyukhtai Cave
18,000

Malaya Siya
34,000

Mal'ta
21,000

Teshik Tash

Zhoukoudian
25,000

Zasaragi 50,000

bilisi
Yerevan
skhul
90,000
Shanidar
Mount Carmel

Lantian

Yunxian

Langtandong

Qafzeh
90,000

Linjiang
67,000?

Okinawa
32,000

Tham Khuyen

Narmada

adar
Middle Awash

Omo 130,000
Koobi Fora
West Turkana

Olduvai Gorge

Laetoli

Tabon
24–22,000

Niah Cave 40,000

SUNDA
land bridge

Wadjak 50–25,000

Bobangara 38,000

bwe

Sangiran
Trinil Solo

SAHUL
land bridge

kapansgat
rtkrans
rder Cave
5,000

Devil's Lair
34,000

Lake Mungo 33,000

Kow Swamp 14,000

Bluff Rockshelter 30,500

Curriculum Context

Students should be aware that the details of human evolution are incomplete.

Over 3 million years ago Africa was home to early hominids, *Australopithecus afarensis*. They foraged on edible roots and meat scavenged from dead animals. Their upright walking position allowed them to keep a lookout for animal predators in open country.

blunt end of the stone would smash stone or bone. *Homo habilis* left so many choppers of so many different sizes and types that their output is known as the Olduwan Industry.

Homo habilis lived only in Africa. It was a later species, *Homo erectus*, that migrated out of Africa and spread across Eurasia. *Homo erectus* lived from 1.85 million years ago until about 400,000 years ago and made tools that were more sophisticated than those of its predecessors. The manufacturing technique, however, was the same: striking one stone against another. The earliest tools associated with *Homo erectus* were found in Olduvai Gorge and are about 1.4 million years old. They are referred to as the Acheulian Industry. Flint was the preferred stone of *Homo erectus*, but flint is not found everywhere. When flint was not available, the Acheulian toolmakers used other rocks, including quartz. Flint and quartz are both varieties of silica, which is silicon dioxide (SiO_2).

Flint

An extremely hard type of black quartz found in sedimentary rocks.

Inventing the hammer

Instead of shaping one stone by striking identical stones together, Acheulian toolmakers used stone hammers to make cleavers and hand axes, with longer, straighter cutting edges than the old choppers. By about 1 million years ago they had discovered a new technique—using hammers made from deer antlers. This development allowed them to work with greater precision to make a much wider range of tools for cutting, drilling, shaping, and hammering.

Neanderthal people (*Homo sapiens neanderthalensis*) lived in Europe, the Mediterranean region, and parts of the Middle East at the same time as modern humans and in some places side by side with them. They first appeared about 100,000 years ago, and they became extinct about 30,000 years ago. Neanderthals made a variety of stone tools, but their simple techniques failed to advance.

Curriculum Context

Students should understand that people continue to invent new ways of doing things.

Modern humans, *Homo sapiens*, were making much more efficient tools by around 40,000 years ago. The Périgordian and Aurignacian industries, named for the two sites in France where evidence for them has been found, produced up to 80 different kinds of stone implements. People were also making tools with stone blades fixed to bone or antler handles. Cro-Magnon people (Cro-Magnon is a rock shelter in southern France), living from 35,000 to 10,000 years ago, made beautifully engraved bone tools that were probably used for ceremonial purposes. Among many other things, they made chisels, awls, and tools with blades for scraping animal skins to make leather. In parts of southwestern France between 21,000 and 17,000 years ago, workers in the Solutrean Industry were producing blades shaped like willow and laurel leaves.

Archaeological remains

Stone tools survive indefinitely, which is why many archaeologists are able to trace their development, but humans have always used other materials, such as wood and plant fibers, that decompose and disappear soon after they are thrown away. Arrowheads and spearheads had wooden shafts, and arrows needed wooden bows to fire them.

People also wore clothes—clothed figures are depicted in early cave art. The first garment may have been a skirt made from cords hung from a belt, worn by women. It is likely that people were twisting fibers into cord and ropes by 20,000 years ago. By that time they were

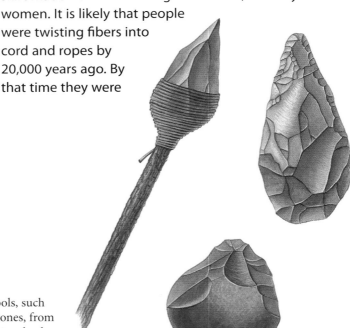

Archaeologist

A person who finds out how people used to live by uncovering and examining the material remains of past societies.

Early humans made basic tools, such as spearheads and cutting stones, from flint. The earliest technique involved striking one stone against another.

also weaving pliable willow stalks to make baskets and fish traps and using twisted cords to make fishing nets. It is a fairly small step from there to making cloth by applying the same technique. The earliest evidence of basket weaving, using palm leaves, split reeds, and other plant fibers, dates from about 5000 B.C. at Fayoum, Egypt. By about 2700 B.C. silk was being woven into cloth in China.

Boats and fishing

Fish were an important part of the diet of most communities, and everyone needed fresh water for drinking, cooking, washing, and processing fibers. Where the nearby river or creek was small and shallow, hunters could wade across it to set traps and spear fish. Wider and deeper rivers and lakes called for an alternative method of hunting for food. A rock carving from northern Europe, made between 9,000 and 10,000 years ago, shows what appears to be a boat carrying hunters in pursuit of reindeer that are swimming across a river. The boat seems to have a frame, in which case it would have resembled the traditional Inuit kayak, the Irish curragh, and the English coracle, which consist of a strong wooden frame covered in animal skin.

Rock carving

The depiction of animals, figures, and abstract design on a rock surface.

Northern Europe was still emerging from the most recent glaciation 10,000 years ago, and the vegetation was tundra rather than the coniferous forests that appeared later. The hunters would have had an abundant supply of small timber but there would have been very few trees big enough to make dugout boats by hollowing out a trunk. The earliest boat of this type known in Europe was found at Pesse in the Netherlands. It is made from pine and is approximately 8,000 years old. Parts of three boats built from planks found at Ferriby Sluice on the southern side of the Humber Estuary in eastern England have been dated at 2,900 years old.

Curriculum Context

Students should understand that ice ages had dramatic effects on the environment.

Making fire

Capturing and making fire changed the lifestyle of early humans. It gave them warmth, a means of defense, and allowed them to settle in previously inhospitable areas. Cooking food enabled them to expand their diet and grow stronger. Sitting around the warmth of a fire, people were also able to develop communication skills that advanced their mental and social development.

Fire was essential for the growth of civilization. People used it to cook their food, warm their homes, clear land for cultivation, make pottery, and eventually smelt metals from ores. Historians usually give credit for the first use of fire, around 750,000 B.C., to *Homo erectus*, a species of early hominids who lived between 1.85 million and 400,000 years ago.

Curriculum Context

Students should be aware that the details of human evolution are incomplete.

Early humans saw how lightning set fire to dry trees and grass and, in some parts of the world, observed vegetation become ignited by molten lava or hot ashes from volcanoes. At first people probably simply "captured" fire from these natural occurrences. They then kept a campfire burning nonstop, day and night. They may have kept glowing coals or charcoal in a brazier; later people would keep a lamp or a candle burning all the time so that they were never without a source of fire. It was much easier to keep a fire going than to start a new one.

Charcoal

A form of carbon made by charring wood in a container, from which air is excluded.

Early methods
In fact, making fire is difficult, and all early methods relied on friction, by rubbing two pieces of wood together until they got hot enough to start a fire. The techniques included the use of fire sticks and fire drills. A fire stick is a stick of dry wood, one end of which has a blunt point that is rapidly turned in a small hollow dug in a larger piece of wood. The stick can be rotated between the palms of a person's hands by rubbing the

palms together back and forth very rapidly. The friction between the two pieces of wood gradually raises them to burning temperature, and the resulting heat ignites pieces of dry grass (tinder) in the hollow. The stick-and-groove method is a variation on the fire-stick idea, in which a fire stick is rubbed hard back and forth along a groove in another piece of wood.

Alternatively, a bow can be used to rotate the fire stick, and that is the principle behind the fire drill. The string of the bow makes a couple of turns around the fire stick, which spins first one way and then the other as the bow is pulled backward and forward.

Early humans also created fire by using sparks produced when a piece of flint strikes a piece of pyrite (a mineral form of iron sulfide). The sparks fall on tinder, and vigorous blowing then causes the smoldering tinder to burst into flame. A tinder box—which was in use for more than 2,000 years—holds all the necessary equipment: flint, steel to strike it on, and tinder (usually moss or dry feathers) to get the fire going.

Another method of making fire used a lens or curved mirror to focus and concentrate the Sun's rays. However, the final breakthrough in fire production came with the invention of matches, but this did not happen until 19th-century developments in chemistry.

Fire-making Machine

The fire drill was probably one of the earliest human inventions. It uses a wooden bow to rotate a blunt-ended fire stick in a hollow in a piece of softer dry wood. The stick spins first one way and then the other as the bow is pulled back and forth, heating the end of the stick.

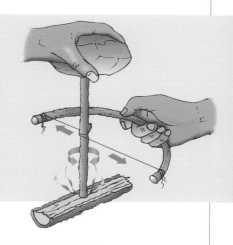

Origin of cereals

There are more than 75,000 species of edible plants in the world, but 60 percent of the world's food comes from just three: wheat, corn, and rice. How did these come to be so important?

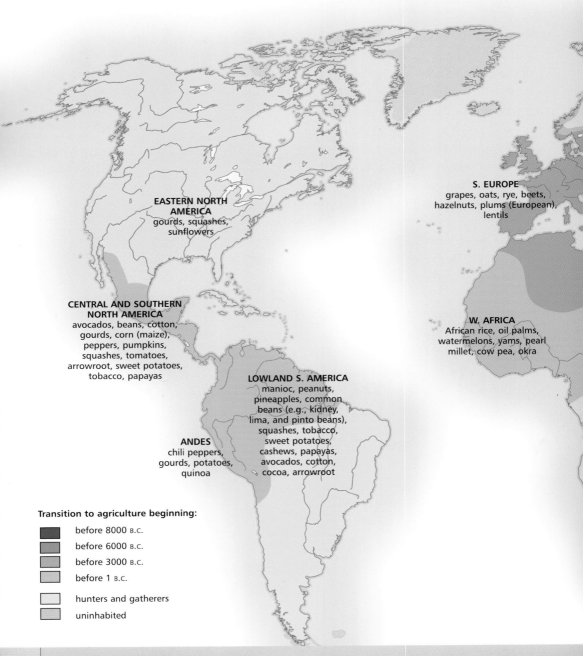

EASTERN NORTH AMERICA
gourds, squashes, sunflowers

S. EUROPE
grapes, oats, rye, beets, hazelnuts, plums (European), lentils

CENTRAL AND SOUTHERN NORTH AMERICA
avocados, beans, cotton, gourds, corn (maize), peppers, pumpkins, squashes, tomatoes, arrowroot, sweet potatoes, tobacco, papayas

W. AFRICA
African rice, oil palms, watermelons, yams, pearl millet, cow pea, okra

LOWLAND S. AMERICA
manioc, peanuts, pineapples, common beans (e.g., kidney, lima, and pinto beans), squashes, tobacco, sweet potatoes, cashews, papayas, avocados, cotton, cocoa, arrowroot

ANDES
chili peppers, gourds, potatoes, quinoa

Transition to agriculture beginning:
- before 8000 B.C.
- before 6000 B.C.
- before 3000 B.C.
- before 1 B.C.
- hunters and gatherers
- uninhabited

Humans evolved as hunter-gatherers. Our ancestors ate plant material collected from the wild, but wild food now makes up only a tiny proportion of what we eat. Domestic plants differ from their wild relatives in that they have undergone a period of rapid evolution in response to artificial selection by humans.

Imagine Italy without tomatoes and Florida without oranges! In the age of global cuisine it can be difficult to appreciate that at the end of the last ice age most crops were still found only in their native ranges, as shown here.

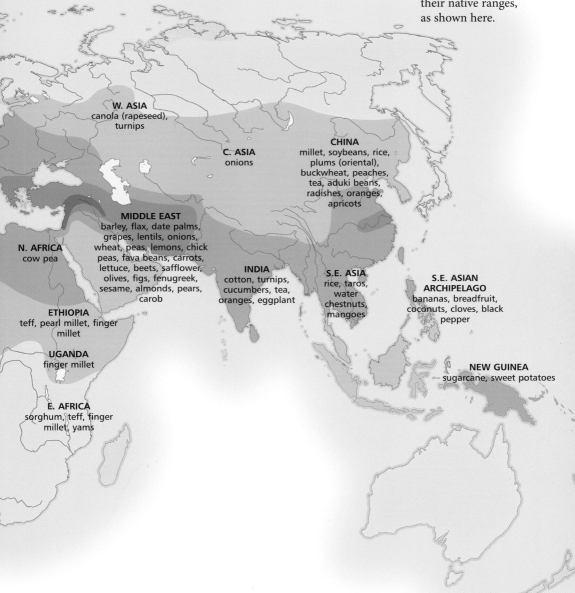

W. ASIA
canola (rapeseed), turnips

C. ASIA
onions

CHINA
millet, soybeans, rice, plums (oriental), buckwheat, peaches, tea, aduki beans, radishes, oranges, apricots

MIDDLE EAST
barley, flax, date palms, grapes, lentils, onions, wheat, peas, lemons, chick peas, fava beans, carrots, lettuce, beets, safflower, olives, figs, fenugreek, sesame, almonds, pears, carob

N. AFRICA
cow pea

INDIA
cotton, turnips, cucumbers, tea, oranges, eggplant

S.E. ASIA
rice, taros, water chestnuts, mangoes

S.E. ASIAN ARCHIPELAGO
bananas, breadfruit, coconuts, cloves, black pepper

ETHIOPIA
teff, pearl millet, finger millet

UGANDA
finger millet

NEW GUINEA
sugarcane, sweet potatoes

E. AFRICA
sorghum, teff, finger millet, yams

The characteristics we prefer, such as large size, flavor, and productivity, are not the same as those favored by natural selection, and most domestic plants are now entirely reliant on humans for survival.

Curriculum Context

The curriculum requires an understanding of the biology of plant reproduction.

The first farmers

Early steps toward agriculture probably involved an awareness of sustainability. Plant gatherers would have understood that if they dug up and ate an entire plant, it was gone forever. But if they collected part of it or waited until it had cast seed before harvesting it, they could come back for more in the future.

The development of modern wheat took thousands of years and benefited from natural mutations and hybridization events. This illustration shows the sequence of events. Modern domestic wheat would not survive well in the wild. Its seeds are too heavy and well attached to disperse, and it struggles to compete with wild varieties.

One of the difficulties in relying on wild plants for food is that they are often spread over a large area and grow mixed in with other, less useful plants. The first deliberate attempts at cultivation appear to have taken place in the Middle East about 10–11,000 years ago (9000–8000 B.C.) in what is known as the Fertile Crescent, an area of land running from the Nile Delta up the eastern coast of the Mediterranean and across present-day Iraq to the Gulf of Persia. People began to sow some of the grain they collected from wild barley and wheat close to home, to make it easier to collect the grain the following year. There is evidence that cultivation of rice began in China in around 6500 B.C. or a little later. The switch from gathering to cultivation made it possible for people to abandon the hunter-gatherer lifestyle in favor of a more sedentary, more predictable, and therefore more secure way of life.

Selective cultivation

With regard to wheat, a natural mutation had produced a variety of wheat known as einkorn, in which the seed head was unusually stable. In wild wheat the seeds are loosely attached, and

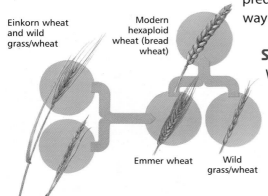

Einkorn wheat and wild grass/wheat

Modern hexaploid wheat (bread wheat)

Emmer wheat

Wild grass/wheat

the heads disintegrate easily. This is beneficial to wild plants because it allows the seeds to be dispersed. But under cultivation the opposite is true. Seeds that disperse are lost. Only the seeds that remain attached to the seed head are harvested, and it is from those seeds that the next year's crop will be sown. So from the start farmers were selecting for stable-headed varieties, reinforcing a process that had begun naturally.

Around 8,000 years ago in the Fertile Crescent an einkorn wheat hybridized naturally with another species of wild grass, forming emmer wheat. Emmer wheat grains were gluten rich and made good flour. In time, another natural mutation occurred that made it easier to separate the grain from the chaff by threshing. Because it made life easier for farmers, it gave the new variety (known as durum wheat) a strong advantage over other types. Modern wheat, the kind used to make most bread, arose from another hybridization, in which emmer wheat crossed with a wild species.

Cereal crops were the first to be cultivated systematically. Barley and wheat were probably first, then rice and corn. Next, between 8,000 and 5,000 years ago, came root crops and legumes, such as beets and beans. Later still were fruiting trees, leafy vegetables, and crops grown for feeding livestock. By 2,000 years ago specialized crops such as medicinal and cooking herbs were under cultivation. Some plants even began to be domesticated simply for their decorative value. The process continues to this day, although most recent domestications have been on a relatively small scale, such as the development of ornamental or novelty plants.

Weeds and Competition

Before the cultivation of crops there was no such thing as a weed. But domestic plants struggle to compete with wild types. (Wild plants are less productive but much hardier, having been refined by competition over many generations.) Today farmers strive to ensure that domestic varieties face little or no competition by removing any plant that threatens to overrun a crop or compete with it for nutrients or water.

Development of the wheel

The wheel has been invented and reinvented several times throughout history. The details of its first appearance, at least 5,000 years ago, are lost in the distant past, and opinion is divided on exactly how the original invention might have happened.

Six thousand years ago humans were already using drag technology such as plows, sledges, and travois (contraptions made up of two trailing poles for dragging heavy loads). In some parts of the world, heavy objects such as rocks and boats were moved using log rollers. As the object moved forward, rollers were taken from behind and replaced in front. Rollers may have been the starting point for the invention of the cartwheel, and it is easy enough to imagine how this might have happened. At some point it seems likely that someone combined the use of a sledge with the rolling logs.

After a set of logs had been used for some time, they would become worn where they scraped against the sledge. Eventually the sledge would settle into the worn section of the rollers, and maybe this gave people the idea of the axle wheel. The significance of the axle is that, because it has a small circumference, it takes less energy to turn than a whole wheel. A relatively small amount of energy spent turning an axle is magnified into the turning of a large wheel.

But there are problems with the roller theory—whole logs split and fall apart quite easily when rolled under pressure, and tall, straight trees were not abundant in the Middle East, where the first solid evidence for transport wheels appears.

The development of a wheel constructed to rotate on a fixed axle is used by archaeologists as an indicator of

Curriculum Context

Students should understand the concept that energy is conserved.

Potters' turntables are the earliest known use of the wheel, providing a steadily rotating base to create evenly shaped pots and jars.

relatively advanced civilization. The earliest evidence of axled wheels dates back to about 3200 B.C. The Sumerian people of Mesopotamia (modern-day Iraq) produced many pictures of carts with solid wheels, apparently made from two pieces of plank bracketed together and cut into a circular shape. The axles went through the center of each wheel and were fixed in place by lynchpins.

Wheels of war

Similar wheels appeared on war chariots also built by the Sumerians in Mesopotamia in about 2500 B.C. No doubt such vehicles gave armies a huge advantage,

Sumerians

People who lived in the south of Mesopotamia as far south as the Persian Gulf.

but they would still have been very heavy and difficult to control. About 500 years later the Sumerians also developed spoked wheels, which made chariots much lighter and more maneuverable. Over the next 500 years the design spread and was refined by other civilizations, including the Egyptians and the Romans.

War has long been a driving force of invention, and the wheel may be another example of this. The Sumerians were the first to develop wheeled chariots, closely followed by the ancient Egyptians.

Different civilizations may have come up with the wheel independently. In China, for example, the wheel appeared in about 2800 B.C. The Chinese also appear to have been the first to develop the wheelbarrow, around 100 A.D. It was several centuries before European technology caught up—a 13th-century stained glass window in Chartres Cathedral in northern France shows the earliest depiction of a wheelbarrow in the Western world.

Pulleys, millstones, and spinning wheels

However, the first wheels were probably not intended for transportation. Evidence from around 3500 B.C. shows that potters were using simple turntables to help them create smooth, evenly shaped pots. These early potters' wheels were developed further by the Greeks and Egyptians into flywheels that could convert pulses of energy, such as the pressing of a treadle, into smooth, continuous motion. The flywheel was to become just as important as the vehicular wheel. The Greeks also came up with other crucial variations on the wheel. The 4th and 3rd centuries B.C. saw the development of cogs, gearwheels, and pulleys. The waterwheel was another important variation on the basic axled design. First developed around 85 B.C., waterwheels allowed humans to harness the power of water to drive heavy machinery, namely millstones for grinding grain.

Flywheel

A heavy wheel that resists changes in speed and therefore helps steady the rotation of a shaft.

Since ancient times there have been several more wheel innovations. The Chinese began using spinning wheels for manufacturing yarn between 500 and 1000 A.D., and the same development reached Europe several hundred years later, early in the 13th century. The spinning wheel is a variation on the flywheel: As the wheel turns, it rotates a spindle that twists fibers together to make thread many times faster than can be done by hand.

Curriculum Context

Students should be aware that technology has advanced at different times in history.

Entering the machine age

The flywheel also played a crucial role in the Industrial Revolution. When connected to pistons driven by a steam engine, it converted pulses of raw power into smooth movement that could be used to drive machines in mills and factories and, of course, to power locomotives. Later still came wheel-based innovations including turbines, gyroscopes, and castor wheels—all variations on a 5,000-year-old piece of technology that is still going strong today.

One of the Aztec stone "toys" found by Charnay in 1880. It shows that the ancient civilization of the New World understood the concept of the wheel. The mystery remains: Why did they never build full-size versions?

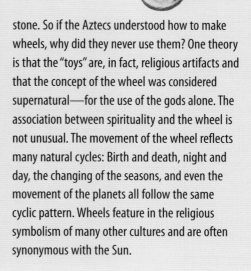

The Supernatural Wheel

Most evidence suggests that the wheel was an Old World technology. Archaeologists are intrigued by the apparent lack of wheels used for transport or machinery by the otherwise advanced ancient civilizations of the New World before European settlers arrived in the 16th century. It seems amazing that people as technologically advanced as the Mayans and the Aztecs failed to come up with their own version of the wheel. In fact, there is some evidence that they did. In 1880 the French explorer Claude-Joseph Désiré Charnay (1828–1915) discovered a collection of what appear to be wheeled toys at Tenenepanco on Mount Popocatépetl (Mexico). They date to about 1500 B.C. and are carved from stone. So if the Aztecs understood how to make wheels, why did they never use them? One theory is that the "toys" are, in fact, religious artifacts and that the concept of the wheel was considered supernatural—for the use of the gods alone. The association between spirituality and the wheel is not unusual. The movement of the wheel reflects many natural cycles: Birth and death, night and day, the changing of the seasons, and even the movement of the planets all follow the same cyclic pattern. Wheels feature in the religious symbolism of many other cultures and are often synonymous with the Sun.

Domestication of animals

There is a big difference between taming an animal and domestication. Taming involves taking an animal from the wild and training it to some extent. Domestic animals are born and bred only in captivity and are descended from a line of captive animals quite distinct from their wild ancestors. Typically they are bigger, fatter, and less intelligent, and they are certainly less able to survive in the wild.

Ancient humans hunted the wild ancestors of modern livestock for thousands of years. Before that our ancestors would have scavenged from the carcasses of dead animals. As humankind evolved, we found different uses for animals. A carcass was no longer merely a source of food but also of other useful materials: fur, hide, sinew, horn, and bone.

The first domesticates

The domestication of livestock probably began about 10,000 years ago (8000 B.C.) when goats and mouflon (sheep), followed by wild pigs (7000 B.C.), were taken into captivity in East Asia and Mesopotamia. It's easy to imagine how it happened. Young animals would have been taken after their mother was killed in a routine hunt and kept captive close to home until they grew to a useful size. It would also have been worth keeping fully grown animals alive because that way their meat would stay fresh.

By about 8,500 years ago (6500 B.C.) cattle were kept under domestication in Africa and India. Chickens were domesticated in Southeast Asia in about 5500 B.C. Other uses for captive animals, as sources of milk, blood, and wool, for example, would have followed. There is also evidence that by about 4000 B.C., people

Curriculum Context

The curriculum requires an awareness that diverse cultures have contributed to technological advances.

Ancient Egyptians were among the first to rear domesticated animals. Images of shepherding are carved into the walls of their tombs; this one dates back to 2000 B.C.

in the Middle East were harnessing the strength of animals to perform hard labor—dragging heavy loads or pulling plows. At the same time in Europe horses began to be kept. To begin with they would have provided just meat and milk, but within a relatively short time people were riding them—some 6,000-year-old horse teeth found in the Ukraine show signs of wear that may have been caused by a bit. By 2000 B.C. horses were animals of status, ridden by wealthy or important people. They were also used in war to intimidate the enemy, ridden by cavalry soldiers or pulling chariots. Bactrian camels were domesticated in Afghanistan by about 2500 B.C. In the New World the llama was domesticated in about 3000 B.C., and the guinea pig (cavy) in 2000 B.C. The latter was bred for meat in South America long before it became a pet.

Choosing an animal

Some animals are better suited to domestication than others. Relatively few species possess all the qualities that make a good domesticate. Some of the main requirements are a matter of simple economics. The cheapest and easiest animals to keep are grazers such as cattle and sheep. They simply need to be turned out to forage for themselves. Goats and camels are equally easy but need a closer eye kept on them because they will eat just about anything. Horses, on the other hand, need to be provided with grain as well as grass. This makes them more expensive to keep and explains why they were domesticated later than other livestock. Another economic consideration is the speed at which an animal grows and matures. From a farmer's perspective only animals that reach a useful size and reproductive maturity quickly are worth keeping.

Other considerations relate to the animal's behavior. Temperament is important. Cattle and horses are far more easily handled than zebras and hippopotamuses, for example, and sheep and pigs are less panicky than

Carnivores—a Special Case for Cats and Dogs

Carnivores in general are expensive to feed, and most are antisocial and potentially dangerous. Dogs are domesticated wolves. As such they are good scavengers and highly social. Their intelligence and loyalty make them uniquely useful. There is reliable evidence that dogs lived in association with humans as early as 12,000 years ago (10,000 B.C.) in Mesopotamia and at least 11,000 years ago (9000 B.C.) in North America. The relationship probably began as a hunting partnership. Cats, however, are solitary creatures and do not fit the profile of typical domesticates. Their relationship with humans began when, as opportunistic predators, they began exploiting the populations of rats and mice thriving in human settlements of the Middle East about 7,000 years ago (5000 B.C.). No doubt their pest control services were welcome, but they remained very much wild animals. It was religion that finally brought the cat under domestication about 4,500 years ago (2400 B.C.) in Egypt, where they were considered to be sacred. The status of domestic cats has remained unusual—even the tamest house cat retains a certain degree of independence from humans, and millions of them return to a wild existence every year.

deer and antelope. Animals that are stressed in captivity tend not to breed well. Another characteristic shared by successfully domesticated animals is the tendency to form social groups. The wild ancestors of domesticates all live in groups with a hierarchical structure. They are used to having a leader, and so it has been relatively easy for them to submit to human dominance.

In many cases the wild species from which domestic animals have evolved are now extinct. Today, there are no pure-bred wild horses, dromedary camels, llamas, or guinea pigs, only feral ones descended from escaped domestics or deliberate reintroductions. The last wild aurochs (the ancestor of domestic cattle) were killed in 1627 A.D. Wild Bactrian camels and wild yak are highly endangered. And there is no such thing as a wild alpaca and probably never has been—it seems this long-haired cousin of the llama may have evolved under domestication, perhaps through hybridization between llamas and wild vicuna.

Extinct

A species of animal or plant that no longer exists.

Writing and numbers

People have always needed to keep records of important events, goods stored or traded, and taxes collected. A drawing is the simplest type of record. Scientists believe that the cave paintings in the Lascaux Grotto in France, made between 17,000 and 15,000 years ago and depicting various animals and a man, record a religious ritual. Early drawings signified exactly what they represented—a picture of a deer meant "deer." Gradually, the symbols acquired more abstract meanings, and eventually they developed into writing.

From pictures to letters

Writing developed as a way of keeping records. At first, representational drawings became simpler in form. "Sun" might be a small circle inside a larger circle, and water might be depicted as a wavy line. Such simple signs could be drawn quickly and remained clearly recognizable even when they were made very small. In time they came to have more than one meaning. The sign for "Sun" also meant "day," or in Egypt the Sun-god Re (or Ra).

In the next stage each sign came to represent a sound as well as an object, or simply a sound. This type of writing, in which pictures represent sounds, is called "hieroglyphic," and the best-known type was developed in Egypt, where it first appeared around 3100 B.C. By about 2700 B.C. Egyptian hieroglyphic writing had been more or less standardized and it remained in use for some 3,000 years.

Cuneiform

At about the same time another system of writing was emerging in Mesopotamia, the region lies between the Euphrates and Tigris rivers, in what is present-day Iraq. While this also began as a system of stylized pictures, it developed very differently than Egyptian hieroglyphics, because of the tools used to write it.

Whereas Egyptian scribes wrote on papyrus paper with reed pens and ink, Mesopotamian scribes pressed a writing tool called a stylus into a tablet of soft clay, making a wedge or round shape. This type of writing is called cuneiform. It came into use in about 2400 B.C. Cuneiform was the writing system used by the Sumerians, the Assyrians, and the Babylonians. It spread to Persia and remained in use for nearly 2,000 years.

A preserved Babylonian clay tablet from the 7th century B.C., showing cuneiform text.

Alphabets

The first real alphabet (the Proto Canaanite) emerged in the Middle East in about 1700 B.C. It used 30 symbols to represent single sounds. From this the Phoenician alphabet of 22 letters developed by about 1000 B.C., eventually giving rise to Arabic, Hebrew, Latin, and Greek scripts.

Chinese writing also developed from pictures. They were inscribed on bones and seashells that were then thrown into the air. People believed that the pattern in which they fell conveyed messages from the gods or from dead ancestors. These symbols were in use from about 1700 B.C. They became more abstract during the Zhou Dynasty (about 1122–256 B.C.).

Keeping records

Record keepers also needed a way to write numbers. A picture of one cow can represent one cow, but it would be impractical to represent 60 cows by drawing each one. In about 30,000 B.C. in what is now the Czech Republic, someone carved 55 notches (11 groups of five) on a bone from the leg of a wolf. They may refer to the number of animals killed in a hunt, although no one really knows, but it is clearly a numerical record. A stick or bone used in this way is called a tally stick.

Curriculum Context

The curriculum expects students to understand that mathematics plays an essential role in all aspects of an inquiry and for accurately measuring change.

Numerals for quantities greater than ten were first used in Egypt in about 3400 B.C., Mesopotamia in about 3000 B.C., and in Crete in about 1200 B.C. Using ten as a base was an obvious choice because humans have ten fingers, and most cultures adopted this counting system. The Babylonians and Sumerians were the major exceptions: They calculated to base 60.

Egyptian and cuneiform numbers used different symbols for 1; 10; 100; 1,000; 10,000; 100,000; and 1,000,000, and indicated higher values by repeating them, as in Roman numerals, where X is 10, XX is 20, and XXX is 30; C is 100, and CCC is 300. However, none of these systems had a symbol for zero.

Babylonian Arithmetic Lives

The arithmetic we use today is to base 10, and the value of a digit depends on its position. For example, 87 is 8 "tens" plus 7 "units." The Babylonians calculated to base 60. They would have written 87 as 1 "sixty" plus 27, or 1 27. It is similar to the way we might write 87 minutes as 1 hour 27 minutes or 1° 27'. This is no coincidence. We have kept the Babylonian base 60 system for hours, minutes, and seconds, and for degrees, minutes, and seconds. There are 360 degrees (six "sixties") in a circle.

Arithmetic books

Clay was plentiful, and cuneiform writing has survived on thousands of Babylonian tablets. As long as the clay remained soft, a tablet could be wiped smooth and used again. It would be discarded once the clay began to set. Some of the surviving tablets were exercise books used by

Proto Canaanite	Early letter names and meanings	Phoenician	Early Greek	Early monumental Latin	Modern English
	alp oxhead		△		A
	bêt house			B	B
	gaml throwstick				C
	digg fish		△	D	D
	hô(?) man calling				E
	wô mace				F
	zê(n) ?	I	I		
	hê(t) fence?			H	H
	tê(t) spindle?				
	yad arm	Z		I	I
	kapp palm			K	K
	lamd ox-goad	C			L
	mêm water				M
	nahs snake				N
	cên eye	O	O	O	O
	pi't corner?				P
	sa(d) plant		M		
	qu(p) ?				Q
	ra's head of man			R	R
	taan composite bow	W			S
	tô owner's mark		X	T	T

Most of the letters in our modern English alphabet can be traced back to the Phoenician alphabet, as shown here. However, the Phoenicians made no distinction between the letter J and the letter I.

Curriculum Context

The curriculum requires an appreciation that through the ages different cultures have come up with different answers to the same needs.

students. They include multiplication tables and complex calculations. Egyptians, on the other hand, used only addition and the two times table. They performed multiplication by repeatedly doubling or halving and then adding the results. Nevertheless, surviving Egyptian papyri describe such tasks as dividing a given number of loaves among a given number of people and finding the area of a right-angled triangle.

Agriculture and food

The history of farming dates from about 11,000 years ago when people gradually gave up the hunter-gatherer way of life and began to form more settled communities. At first using slash-and-burn techniques, people began to live in settlements where they could grow crops and rear animals. The need to store and prepare the food they grew also led to new discoveries.

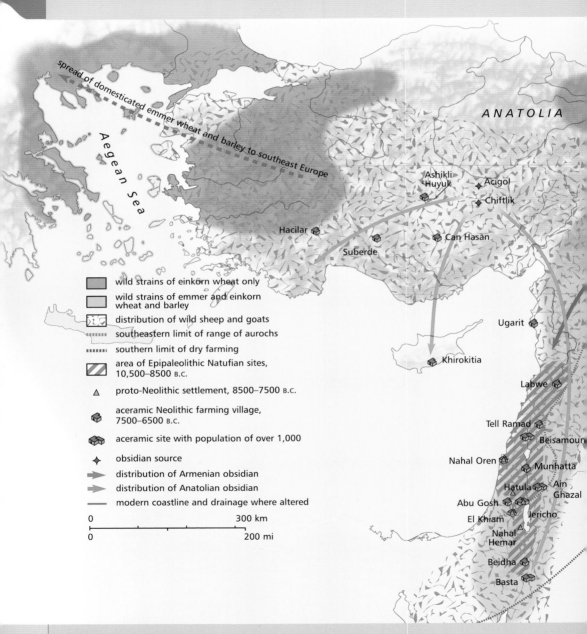

ANATOLIA

Aegean Sea

spread of domesticated emmer wheat and barley to southeast Europe

Ashikli Huyuk
Acigol
Chiftlik
Hacilar
Can Hasan
Suberde

Ugarit

Khirokitia

Labwe

Tell Ramad
Beisamoun
Nahal Oren
Munhatta
Hatula
Ain Ghazal
Abu Gosh
El Khiam
Jericho
Nahal Hemar
Beidha
Basta

▨	wild strains of einkorn wheat only
▢	wild strains of emmer and einkorn wheat and barley
	distribution of wild sheep and goats
····	southeastern limit of range of aurochs
▪▪▪▪	southern limit of dry farming
▨	area of Epipaleolithic Natufian sites, 10,500–8500 B.C.
△	proto-Neolithic settlement, 8500–7500 B.C.
⬡	aceramic Neolithic farming village, 7500–6500 B.C.
⬢	aceramic site with population of over 1,000
✦	obsidian source
➤	distribution of Armenian obsidian
➤	distribution of Anatolian obsidian
—	modern coastline and drainage where altered

0   300 km

0   200 mi

Farming progress

In the fertile valley of the Nile River in Egypt and in Mesopotamia between the rivers Tigris and Euphrates (in present-day Iraq) early farmers used digging sticks and hoes to prepare the soil for planting and sickles to harvest crops. The plow, invented in about 3500 B.C. by

The Fertile Crescent was a region that arched around the Middle East from the Persian Gulf in the southeast to Palestine and Egypt in the southwest. Most of the settlements on the map date from Stone Age times.

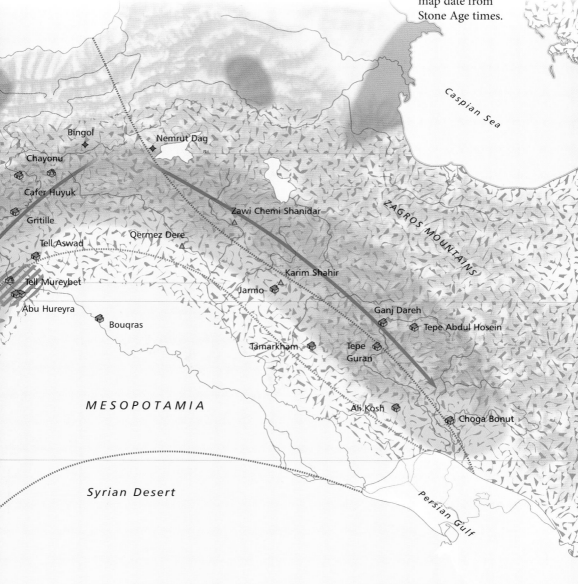

Bingol

Nemrut Dag

Chayonu

Cafer Huyuk

Gritille

Zawi Chemi Shanidar

Qermez Dere

Tell Aswad

Karim Shahir

Tell Mureybet

Jarmo

Abu Hureyra

Ganj Dareh

Bouqras

Tepe Abdul Hosein

Tamarkham

Tepe Guran

ZAGROS MOUNTAINS

Caspian Sea

MESOPOTAMIA

Ali Kosh

Choga Bonut

Syrian Desert

Persian Gulf

This papyrus sheet is from the *Book of the Dead*, an ancient Egyptian Funerary text, and shows a plow being drawn by an ox.

farmers in Mesopotamia and China, greatly extended the areas of land that could be tilled to grow food. Over the years selective breeding resulted in higher-yielding strains of cereal plants such as wheat and barley. People also applied domestication and selective breeding to animals. Beasts of burden, such as horses, oxen, and buffalo, began to replace human muscle power to carry loads, draw plows, and pull carts.

Preserving food

It was difficult to keep food over the winter, although people did store dried grain. Pulses (edible seeds), such as lentils and beans, could also be dried. Farmers slaughtered many of their animals in late fall because they had insufficient food for them over winter. People in early settlements preserved animal carcasses simply

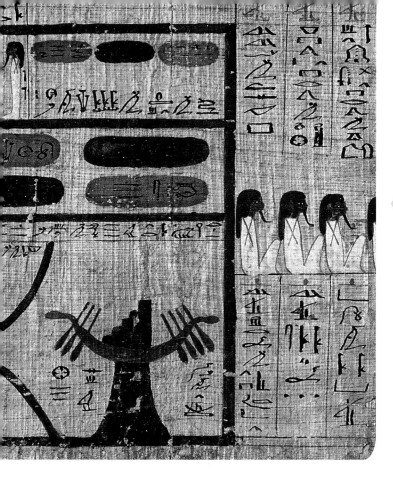

Curriculum Context

Students should understand that diagrams and artwork are an important method of passing on information.

by allowing them to dry in the wind, and in cold climates stored them in caves. New technologies arose from the need to store and preserve food. One food preservation method involved smoking meat or fish over a wood fire, a method still used today (more for flavor than out of necessity). Fish and meat were also salted. A combination of curing (smoking) and salting of pig meat (pork) created ham and bacon.

Curing

Preserving meat for future use, and preventing its deterioration.

People also began to use grindstones to make flour from harvested grains and to make clay pots to store food as well as for cooking. The earliest-known pottery dates from about 11,000 B.C. in Japan. It was invented independently in the Middle East about 5,000 years later. As the potters grew more skillful, they built ovens for baking the clay.

Ancient medicine

People have always fallen sick, and throughout history there have been doctors to heal them. Hammurabi, the king who ruled Babylon from 1792 to 1750 B.C., made many laws. He also issued many judgments that were inscribed on a stone pillar, including penalties for doctors who made mistakes. If a doctor opened an abscess and the patient died, for example, the doctor's hands were to be cut off; but if the patient were a slave, the doctor had only to provide a replacement slave.

Community medicine

Every Babylonian was encouraged to help the sick. It was customary to leave sick people lying in the street so that passers-by could offer advice. Professional doctors often predicted the course of a disease by divination, based on examining the liver of an animal that had been sacrificed.

Seeking the advice of friends and neighbors was a very ancient tradition, found everywhere, and "folk medicine" of that kind is practiced to this day. People who had not yet discovered how the human body is constructed nor how it functions believed there were two classes of illness. Trivial complaints, such as an upset stomach, headache, or cold, were part of everyday life. People put up with them and treated them with whatever remedy seemed to work.

Curriculum Context

Students should be aware that science and technology have greatly improved the health of people.

More serious illnesses, such as fevers, smallpox, or dysentery, were the work of demons that had entered the body or of gods who had been offended. They avenged themselves by throwing darts or worms into the victim's body or by extracting some important part—often the soul. Treatment involved removing the dart, worm, or demon causing the symptoms or encouraging the soul to return to its proper place in the body. Depending on what they considered appropriate, practitioners would use suction or physical manipulation of the patient's body to remove the cause of the disease as well as administering herbal medicines by mouth and performing incantations. Treatment therefore involved magic or religious ritual, and those who performed it were known as "medicine men" or "medicine women."

Drilling a hole 1 to 2 inches (2.5–5 cm) across in the top of the skull was one way to allow whatever caused an illness to escape. This was called trepanning, or trephining, and it was practiced in many parts of the world. Prehistoric trepanned skulls have been found in several parts of Europe and also in Peru. Surprisingly,

Herbal medicine

A medicine made from plants, such as salicylic acid (aspirin) made from the bark of willow.

Traditional Chinese medicine is still practiced, with herbal remedies that are sold by weight.

A 19th century Japanese anatomy chart, showing the channels used for acupuncture.

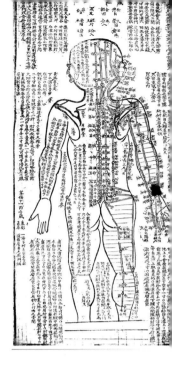

the patient often survived the brutal treatment. In the unearthed ancient skulls, bone has regrown to seal the holes.

The Egyptians also had physicians and surgeons. Imhotep was one of the earliest physicians—and also vizier (civil officer), astrologer, architect, and adviser to King Djoser, who reigned from 2630 to 2611 B.C. Within 100 years of his death, Imhotep became the god of medicine.

Chinese medicine began over 4,500 years ago. Chinese doctors believed that illness was caused by imbalances between the female (yin) and male (yang) cosmic principles, and their treatment aimed to correct the imbalance. Doctors used herbal remedies, such as ma huang (*Ephedra sinica*), which yields ephedrine, a drug that is still used to treat asthma and bronchitis. Perhaps the most famous Chinese medical herb is ginseng (*Panax pseudoginseng*).

Acupuncture was first practiced more than 4,500 years ago. Chinese scientists were forbidden to dissect human bodies, so they had no accurate knowledge of anatomy. They believed the body contained three "burning spaces" and that the cosmic principles (yin and yang) circulate through 12 channels. Acupuncture aims to alter the distribution of yin and yang in the 12 channels and in the burning spaces. The technique involves inserting warm or cold metal needles of varying lengths into the skin at particular points on the body that are related to the organ or organs that are sick. There are hundreds of such points.

Ayurvedic medicine, based on religious writings called the "Vedas," is still used in India, where it probably began about 3,000 years ago. The aim is to prevent illness through modifications of lifestyle, hygiene, and yoga, and to cure complaints by using herbal and mineral preparations and a correct diet. Ayurvedic practitioners treat the whole person rather than simply dealing with a particular illness.

The symbol of the snake

In Greek mythology Asclepius (or Aesculapius) was one of Apollo's many sons. He was raised by Cheiron, the wisest of all the centaurs (creatures that had the body of a horse and the head, torso, and arms of a man). Cheiron taught Asclepius the art of healing, and Greeks worshipped him as the god of healing. Hundreds of temples to Asclepius were built across Greece. They were like hospitals, and sick people visited them seeking cures. Asclepius came to be associated with snakes because he was thought to appear occasionally in the form of a snake. Healing would come about through a visitation by Asclepius (or a snake) in a dream. Patients spent the night at the temple, and the next day described their dreams to the temple priests, who gave them advice about what was needed to cure them.

Asclepius may, in fact, have been a real person. If so, he lived in about 1200 B.C. According to tradition he had two sons, Podalirius and Machaon, both of whom became military surgeons.

A pillar from a Turkish temple to Asclepius, featuring two snakes entwined around olive branches, and the wheel of life between them.

Building the pyramids

The Great Pyramid at Giza, near Cairo in Egypt, is the only one of the Seven Wonders of the Ancient World to survive intact. That it is still standing after 4,500 years is testament to the technological sophistication, ingenuity, and organizational skills of the ancient civilization that built it.

Humankind seems compelled to create tall buildings. Four thousand years ago the only shape for such a structure was a broad base tapering at the top—giving stability and a means of transporting building materials upward. Smooth-sided pyramids seem to have been a natural progression from another type of building, known as a ziggurat. Ziggurats were built by the ancient civilizations of Mesopotamia and Persia (Sumerians, Babylonians, and Assyrians) between 3000 and 500 B.C. A ziggurat was a sort of temple-tower built in several levels, each smaller than the one below. It probably represented a sacred mountain or staircase to the gods, a link between Earth and heaven. Ziggurats were built with a core of unfired mud bricks and an outer covering of fired bricks, often glazed with elaborate colors. They had between two and seven tiers. Among the most famous are the beautifully preserved ziggurat at Ur in Iraq and the ziggurat of Marduk in Babylon, thought to be the building described in the *Bible* as the Tower of Babel.

Pyramid

Any huge structure with a square base and four sloping, triangular sides meeting at the top.

Curriculum Context

Students should be aware that different cultures may independently make similar technological advances.

Refining the design

The first pyramid in Egypt was built at Saqqara, starting in about 2630 B.C., to honor King Djoser (reigned 2630–2611 B.C.). It had a stepped structure not unlike that of a ziggurat, the important difference being that it was made of stone rather than mud. Within 30 years the Egyptians had refined the design and were beginning to build smooth pyramids, such as the Red Pyramid at Dashur, generally regarded as the first "true" pyramid. The core was still made of massive structural blocks but they were cased in smaller blocks to smooth the outline into something that was more pleasing to the eye.

The pyramids were burial structures built to honor the kings (or pharaohs), who were regarded by their people as living gods. The site for a pyramid would have been chosen by the king himself. Detailed plans were drawn up by skilled draftsmen working on sheets of papyrus (paper was not invented until about 105 A.D.). Sometimes the pyramids were built over significant natural features such as rocky outcrops. This meant that fewer materials had to be imported but it

As this cutaway diagram shows, the internal structure of the pyramid was more complex than the outside, with a system of chambers, access tunnels, and air vents.

The internal structure of the pyramids was made from huge blocks of hewn stone. When they were in place, an outer casing of smaller blocks was added. Scaffolding and ramps used to construct the main structure were dismantled as the outer casing was built, working from the apex downward.

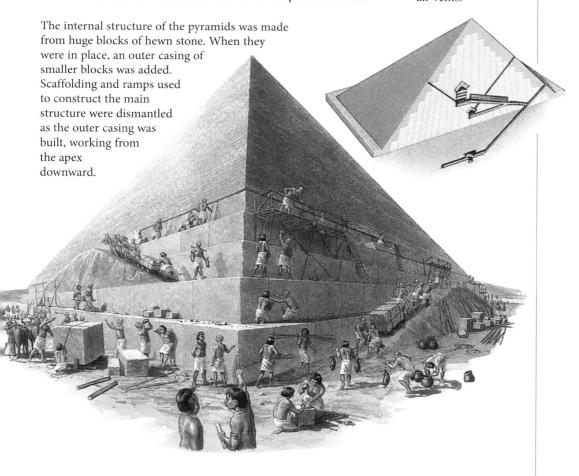

must have caused headaches for the architects, since uneven ground is much more difficult to survey and measure precisely, and precision was imperative.

All Egyptian pyramids are built along a precise north–south axis, but this was achieved thousands of years before the magnetic compass existed. Instead, the Egyptians used a surveying tool called a bay to determine the direction of true north from the stars. The perfection of symmetry in the finished pyramids shows that the Egyptians also had a firm grasp of geometry, allowing them to mark out the base of the pyramid as a perfect square. Anything less than right-angled perfection would mean that the four sides would fail to form a neat point at the apex. The same perfection was required of the individual blocks, the shape of which was honed by skilled masons.

Curriculum Context

The curriculum expects students to be able to use geometry to solve problems.

Ancient mystery

For very many years the questions that have puzzled archaeologists most about the pyramids are: How did the builders transport the enormous blocks of stone used in construction, and how did they raise them to such great heights? The blocks used to build the Great Pyramid at Giza weigh from 2.5 to 15 tons (2–14 tonnes) each, and those at the top have been lifted 480 feet (147 m) above ground level. The answer to the first question is that the stone was quarried as locally as possible. Anything brought from far away was carried by boat along the Nile River. To carry the stone to the top the builders used ramps—gentle gradients up which it would have been possible to drag the blocks on wooden sleds. Once at the top, it is assumed that wooden and bronze levers were used to maneuver the blocks into position.

Curriculum Context

Students should be able to describe the processes used in construction.

The shape of the ramps has been the subject of much debate. It is likely that they would have taken a variety of forms, some straight, others zigzagging up the face,

Which Ramps?

The simplest ramps were built approaching one side of the pyramid. But to maintain a shallow gradient, they would have to have been very long and contain almost as much building material as the

Zigzag ramp

pyramid itself. Other ramp designs, such as zigzags and spirals, use less material but are more complex structurally.

Spiral ramp

A side-on ramp shown growing with the pyramid

and others spiraling around from the base to the summit. These ramps would have been impressive feats of engineering in their own right.

Smaller blocks, such as those used to construct the outer casing of the pyramids, may have been lifted using mechanical devices. The Greek historian Herodotus described such things but not in great detail, and so far there is little archaeological evidence to suggest how they would have worked.

While technology obviously played a key role in the construction of the pyramids, perhaps the real secret of the Egyptians' success was in organizing what must have been a vast workforce. Estimates of the numbers of people involved vary from 100,000 to just a few thousand. In general, the estimates have fallen as our understanding of Egyptian technology and organization has increased. It seems unlikely that these people were slaves. There is good archaeological evidence of thriving communities centered on the construction sites, providing accommodation and services for a huge, highly specialized workforce.

Curriculum Context

The curriculum requires an awareness that science and technology have been practiced by people for a long time.

The first boats

The very first boat was probably a fallen log drifting on a current—ideal for traveling downstream. For increased stability and carrying capacity, people lashed logs together with vines and later ropes to make rafts. Inflated leather bladders or sealed gourds or pots could add buoyancy. Oars or paddles gave people some control over these primitive craft.

The dugout canoe was the first purpose-built boat. It was made from a log hollowed out using an ax or an adz (an ax with the blade at right angles to the shaft). The oldest surviving example of a dugout boat, found in the Netherlands, dates from about 6300 B.C. Next, boatbuilders learned to make a canoe by stretching leather or bark over a light wooden framework, using resin or bitumen to help make it watertight. Native American bark canoes and Welsh coracles use this type of lightweight construction. Oars provided propulsion. The next development was the sail, invented by the Egyptians in about 3500 B.C.

A coracle is a type of circular canoe made by stretching animal skins, often with a thin layer of tar, over a lightweight wooden framework. Legend has it that the Irish monk St. Brendan (484–577 A.D.) navigated a primitive craft like this all the way across the Atlantic Ocean to North America.

Sail development

At first Egyptian boat hulls were made from woven papyrus reeds, but they later (c.4000 B.C.) used wooden planks bound together with strips of leather or papyrus. The first sailboats were square-rigged, with a square sail set at more or less right angles to the direction of travel. They were fine as long as you wanted to go in the same direction as the wind, and were used by the Egyptians, other Mediterranean peoples, and even the Vikings of northern Europe for

A wooden solar barge, which was used in the funerals of Egyptian pharaohs in around 2500 B.C.

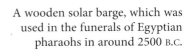

many centuries. The boat was steered using one or two long oars over the stern. The sail was usually wider than it was tall and could be angled slightly using ropes attached to yards at the top and bottom of the sail. There were often raised lookout positions in the bow and stern and a deckhouse for passengers in the center. Some of the boats were very large. A highly decorated dismantled boat found buried near a tomb dating from about 2500 B.C. was 140 feet (43 m) long and constructed from more than 1,200 separate pieces of cedar wood. But perhaps because the square-sailed ship lacked maneuverability, later Egyptian vessels abandoned sails and reverted to banks of oars for propulsion. By about 700 B.C., the Phoenicians were using vessels known as biremes that had two banks of oars; by about 650 B.C., they had progressed to triremes with three banks of oars.

Adding maneuverability

In the 1st century A.D., Chinese boatbuilders invented the rudder, a pivoted vertical plank that is an integral part of the boat.

Phoenicians

A maritime trading culture that spread across the Mediterranean from modern-day Lebanon during the period 1550 B.C. through 300 B.C.

They also invented so-called mat-and-batten sails, with each mast having a set of sails separated by horizontal battens (or yards), still seen today on Chinese junks. Another major breakthrough was the triangular lateen sail, invented in about the 3rd century by Arabian sailors. A lateen sail can be swung through an angle to allow the vessel to sail "closer to the wind"; in other words, the wind does not have to come from directly behind the ship for it to make reasonable progress. Most Arab dhows today still carry triangular sails; using similar vessels, the Arabs explored the eastern coast of Africa south to the Cape and possibly beyond.

Exploring the oceans

Mediterranean vessels also adopted lateen sails, often in combination with square sails on the main masts. For example, a caravel has four masts with square sails on the first two masts and triangular sails on the other two. It was the descendants of these craft that later Spanish and Portuguese navigators sailed on their epic voyages of exploration, becoming the first vessels to circumnavigate the globe.

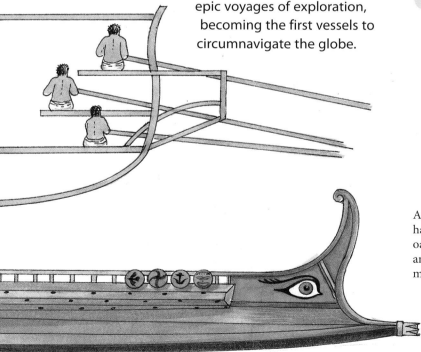

A Persian trireme had three banks of oars for propulsion and a rudder for maneuverability.

Using metals

Mycenae was a prehistoric city on the mainland of southern Greece to the west of Athens. The poet Homer described it as "golden." When European archaeologists excavated the many graves at Mycenae in the 19th century, they discovered bronze swords, a dagger, and other elaborate grave goods. One of the most beautiful items is a gold cup, called the Cup of Nestor, dating from 1600 to 1500 B.C.

Mycenae was once ruled by Agamemnon, the king who attacked Troy, which was ruled by Priam. Archaeologists excavating at the site of Troy found a grave dating from no later than 2000 B.C., containing what they called "Priam's treasure." This included jewels, gold plate, and ornaments, all held in a silver cup.

Lapis lazuli

A blue semiprecious stone.

The Egyptians also produced gold ornaments. The mask of Tutankhamun, the boy king who reigned from 1333 to 1323 B.C., is made from gold inlaid with lapis lazuli. It was found in his tomb. Gold and silver vessels, masks, ceremonial weapons, and ornaments have been found in graves throughout the eastern Mediterranean region and Near East. By about 1600 B.C., Mycenaean metalworkers were making daggers with bronze blades inlaid with gold, electrum (an alloy of silver and gold), silver, and niello (a black substance made from sulfur mixed with silver, lead, or copper).

Curriculum Context

Students should understand that producing objects can require the skills of cutting, shaping, treating, and joining common materials, such as metal.

Sources of metals

Gold, silver, and copper occur "native." That is to say, nuggets of the metal can be prized from rocks or found lying on the surface or in the sand and gravel of

One of the most famous examples of early decorative metal use is the elaborate funeral mask of Tutankhamun, Egypt's boy-pharaoh, who died in 1324 B.C. aged only 18. It is made of solid gold and inlaid with glass and semi-precious stones.

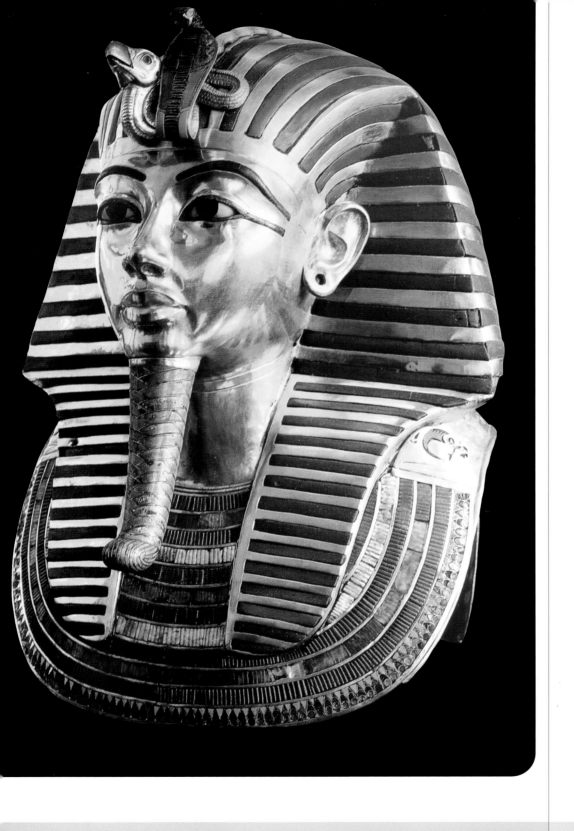

A bronze helmet in the Boetian or Corinthian style, once worn by a Greek soldier. It protects the head, with openings only for the eyes and mouth. Originally there would have been a tall horsehair crest on top to make the soldier wearing it look taller.

riverbeds. Small nuggets of gold can be merged together by hammering; but on its own or alloyed with silver to make electrum, gold is too soft for making tools or weapons. Gold and silver were therefore purely decorative.

Copper was different. Hammering does not fuse copper nuggets. In order to make useful articles from copper, the lumps of metal must be melted and then cast in molds. Hammering then hardens the copper, allowing it to be used to make blades with a sharp edge. Weapons and tools were being made from copper in Egypt by 5000 B.C., and copper axes were being made and used in the Balkans before 3000 B.C. It was around then that people discovered, probably by accident, that they produced much more copper if they melted it in the presence of a particular kind of bright blue stone heated to red heat. They had begun to extract a metal from its ore, in this case azurite.

Many ore minerals contain more than one metal, and some time after 4000 B.C., people began to mix a little tin into the copper. At first it may have happened accidentally when metalworkers used stannite, a rare mineral but one that contains copper, tin, and iron. An alloy of copper and tin is called bronze. It is much harder than copper, and bronze implements retain a sharp edge much longer than those made of copper. Bronze was first made in what is now southern Iraq between 3200 and 2500 B.C. Its use spread throughout the Middle East and Europe and probably China. As it did so, the Copper Age gave way to the Bronze Age.

Iron was also available. Certain meteorites are made mainly of iron, and melting them releases the metal.

But meteorites are rare, and it is more difficult to obtain iron from hematite, its most widespread ore. Copper melts at 1,982.12°F (1,083.4°C), and iron melts at 2,795°F (1,535°C)—a temperature that is much harder to achieve. Smelting hematite produces a spongy mass of iron globules mixed with waste products, called slag. Changing this into workable iron requires repeated melting and hammering. Nevertheless, iron was being produced in southern India around 2000 B.C. An iron dagger blade dating from about 2200 B.C. was found at Alaca Hüyük in Anatolia (present-day Turkey), although it was a precious and probably ceremonial object. Iron was becoming important to the Hittites by 1400 B.C., and by 1000 B.C. its use had spread across Europe.

Meteorite

A rock fragment that is of extraterrestrial origin.

Carbon steel

Iron is soft, and an iron sword blade has to be straightened after each blow struck with it, so at first iron could not compete against bronze. Charcoal, an impure form of carbon, was the fuel the smelters used. The smiths discovered that iron is strengthened if kept for a long time at bright-red heat in a charcoal fire. By absorbing carbon from the charcoal, iron is converted into steel, and steel can be made stronger still if it is plunged into water while red hot. Steel was first made in India in about the 3rd century B.C., and was exported widely. Stories about swords with special powers probably refer to steel blades that were tougher and sharper even than bronze.

Curriculum Context

Students should understand that objects can be described by the properties of the materials from which they are made.

Alloys

An alloy is a mixture of two or more metals, often with small amounts of other elements. Alloys are made by isolating the metallic ingredients, mixing the metals in the required proportions, and finally melting the metals together. The properties of an alloy differ from those of the metals that make it. The first alloys were of copper and tin, which make bronze. The finest bronze contains 89 percent copper and 10 percent tin, with very small amounts of other metals.

Calendars

In the 1970s scientists excavating a cave in Swaziland discovered a baboon's leg bone, now called the Lebombo bone, marked with 29 notches. The person who made those marks lived about 35,000 years ago, and the marks probably record the passage of time. If so, it is a "calendar stick," similar to those made until quite recently by many Native American tribes.

Following the Moon

The Lebombo bone is not the only example of an early calendar from Africa. On the shores of Lake Edward in the Democratic Republic of Congo there was once a small fishing and farming community. It was destroyed by a volcanic eruption but it left behind a bone that was discovered in 1960. Known as the Ishango bone after the people who made it, notches on the bone count the days in the lunar cycle, from new Moon to new Moon, over a period of six months. It is thought to date from 25,000 years ago. There are good reasons for predicting the phases of the Moon—for example, hunters can pursue nocturnal animals during the full Moon, and warriors can approach their enemies unnoticed on dark, moonless nights—and the phases are easy to observe. People have also always needed to count the passage of time.

Building a calendar

All early calendars were based on the lunar cycle. The Egyptians were probably the first to develop a complete calendar, extending over a whole year, in about 4236 B.C. It was lunar but it failed to predict the most important event in the Egyptian year—the annual flooding of the River Nile—an event linked to the seasons. Egyptian priest-astronomers found that when the star Sirius was visible shortly before sunrise, the Nile flood followed a few days later. They devised a calendar based on a solar year and lunar months. It had

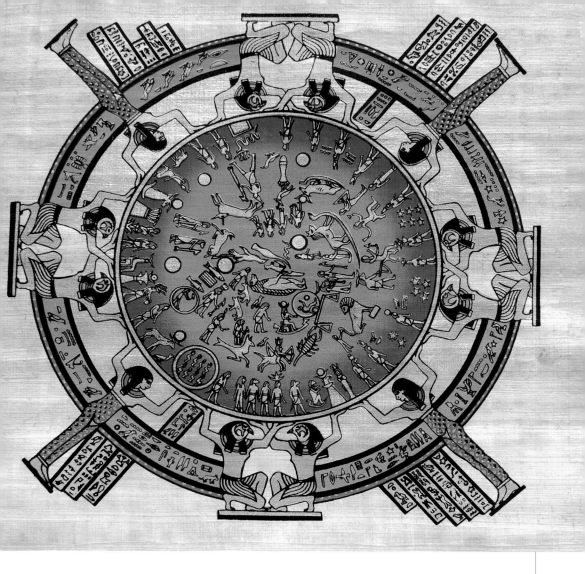

three seasons, each made up of four months of 30 days, with an extra five days at the end of the year, making a year of 365 days. They also used a measurement of time longer than a year: the reign of a king. They counted years as "year such-and-such of king so-and-so."

It was the Egyptians who first divided the day into 24 units. They were not of equal length, however. There were 12 daytime units and 12 nighttime units, and their lengths changed with the seasons.

A blue, ancient Egyptian style of calendar, drawn onto a sheet of papyrus.

By about 3000 B.C., the Sumerians, living in what is now southern Iraq, had devised a calendar that divided the year into 12 months of 30 days each. There were 12 periods in a day, and periods were divided into 30 parts. Throughout the ancient world months began with the first appearance of the new Moon, an event that a high court official would report to the king. Sumerians kept meticulous records, a habit that led them to invent other calendrical measurements. The time an official remained in office was counted in days—as "day such-and-such of A's period as governor."

The Sumerian year began at the time of the barley harvest, but the financial year began about two months later when the harvested grain was sent to the markets. The commencement of the year was a time of religious ritual, when the king would make offerings to the gods of the first fruits of the harvest.

Months and years

Some time before 2100 B.C., Sumerian people began counting lunar years. This was easier than counting days. For example, a loan made in a certain month could be repaid in the same month the following year. This produced a calendar, introduced in about 1800 B.C., with a year that had 12 months alternating between 29 and 30 days. The resulting year of 354 days—(29 x 6) + (30 x 6)—failed to coincide with the agricultural year as measured by the Sun.

To deal with this anomaly, the Sumerians inserted an extra month, but at first the insertion was not standardized across the empire. Each city inserted a month when it was felt necessary. One city might insert an extra 11 months every 18 years, and another might insert two extra months in the same year. The long-term result was the same, but for the purposes of everyday business each city was working to a different calendar.

New Moon

The first visible crescent of the Moon.

Curriculum Context

The curriculum requires an understanding of the role of the Sun in our Solar System.

A Mayan calendar, carved into a stone disk. The ancient Mayan 260-day calendar, which is one of the oldest systems in the world, is still in use in parts of South America.

Sumer was eventually absorbed into the Babylonian Empire, and in the 18th century B.C. the Babylonians adopted the calendar used in the Sumerian city of Nippur. Babylonia occupied the southern half of modern Iraq. The Assyrians occupied the northern half as well as part of southeastern Turkey. Until it grew into a world power, Assyria was a Babylonian dependency, and in about 1100 B.C. the Assyrians adopted the Babylonian calendar.

Other calendars evolve

From about 2950 B.C., the Chinese developed a lunar calendar. Like the Babylonian calendar, it divides the year into 12 months of alternately 29 and 30 days, with additional months added from time to time to keep the calendar in step with the solar year.

The Hindu calendar, introduced around 1000 B.C., divides the year into 12 lunar months of 27 or 28 days, with an additional month inserted every five years. The year is also divided into three periods of four months. The start of each four-month period is marked by a religious festival.

Curriculum Context

Students should understand that different cultures may come up with different answers to the same problem.

Weights and measures

Anybody who buys a pound of rice in Boston, Massachusetts, gets exactly the same amount of rice as somebody who buys a pound of it in London, England. This is because a pound is a standard weight and is (or should be) in many parts of the world. But that has not always been the case.

Curriculum Context

Students should understand that different cultures may come up with different answers to the same problem.

At one time each country had its own system of weights and measures. Even if the names were the same, they often differed greatly. For example, an Irish mile (measuring 2,240 yards, or 2,048 m) was longer

Anubis, the ancient Egyptian god of the afterlife, weighs the heart of a deceased person against the feather of truth. Comparative weight has been used for much longer than standard units.

than an English mile (1,760 yards, or 1,609 m). Yet both are supposedly based on the Roman mile of 1,000 paces (*mille passus* in Latin).

Using hands and feet

People based early measures of length on parts of the body. Thus the Egyptian cubit (about 18 inches, or 45 cm) was the distance from the elbow to the tip of the first finger. It was used from 3500 B.C. The ancient Greek cubit of 1,500 years later was shorter and was based on the length of an average adult's foot (about 12 inches, or 30 cm). The foot (30.5 cm) is still used, and the hand (4 inches, or 10.2 cm) is used to measure

Curriculum Context

The curriculum expects students to use the appropriate units of measure.

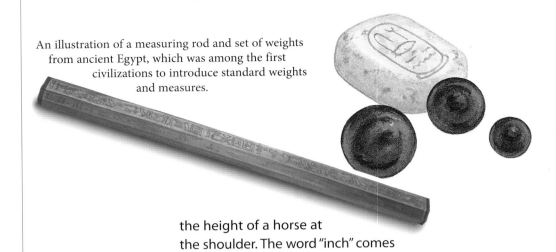

An illustration of a measuring rod and set of weights from ancient Egypt, which was among the first civilizations to introduce standard weights and measures.

the height of a horse at the shoulder. The word "inch" comes from the Latin *uncia*, meaning twelfth part (of a foot).

Weight

Units of weight are more complex because there is no convenient natural object to act as a standard, although we still have the carat (from the Arabic word for a bean) for precious stones (1 carat = 0.007 ounces, or 0.2 g). Grains, based on grains of wheat or rice, have also been used to weigh small amounts for a long time. A modern grain equals 0.0012 ounces (0.05 g), and there are four grains in a carat.

Sumerian traders in about 2500 B.C. made one of the first attempts at standardizing weights with the introduction of the shekel (about 0.3 ounces, or 8.4 g) and the mina, equal to 60 shekels (18 ounces, or 504 g). The oldest surviving example of an actual weight, dating from 2400 B.C., was found at the city of Lagash in Mesopotamia (present-day Iraq). It weighs 16.8 ounces (477 g). About 500 years later the authorities in the Sumerian city of Nippur made a copper bar that acted as a standard of both length and weight. It is 43.4 inches (110.35 cm) long—divided into 4 "feet"—and weighs a massive 91.5 pounds (41.5 kg). The Romans used the *libra pondo* (pound by weight), equal to about 16 ounces (460 g). *Libra* is the origin of the abbreviation "lb" for pound.

Ancient Weights and Measures

Early farmers, craftsmen, engineers, and scientists needed to establish relationships for quantities and dimensions and to record them. But there were no universal systems of weights and measures and (unlike today) no international standards to define them. One standard they did use was the human body, which gave rise to lengths such as the digit (the length of a finger), the palm (the width of a hand), and the foot. But not everyone has the same size of hands or feet—and standards for weight were even more difficult to find. Below is a table listing some of the measures used by early civilizations in the country in which they first appeared.

Unit	Country	Measurement	Modern equivalent	
			(Imperial)	(Metric)
acetabulum	Rome	volume	2.24 fluid ounces	66.41 ml
actus	Rome	area	1,519 sq. yards	0.127 ha
amphora	Greece	volume	10.26 gallons	38.84 l
brachium (arm)	Rome	length	4.6 feet	1.4 m
cab	Israel	volume	4.73 pints	2.24 l
cubit	Egypt	length	17.76 inches	45.11 cm
digit	Egypt	length	0.74 inches	18.72 mm
foot	Babylon	length	13.93 inches	35.4 cm
khoinix	Greece	dry volume	0.98 quarts	1,079 cc
libra (pound)	Rome	weight	1.01 pounds	459.26 g
ligula	Rome	volume	0.39 fluid ounces	11.67 ml
mile	Rome	length	1,618 yards	1,479.5 m
mina	Sumeria	weight	17.7 ounces	504 g
palm (shep)	Egypt	length	2.95 inches	7.49 cm
royal cubit	Egypt	length	20.64 inches	52.42 cm
shekel	Sumeria	weight	0.3 ounces	8.4 g

The digit and the palm were later adopted by ancient Israel, Greece, and Rome with almost exactly the same dimensions. The cubits used in ancient Babylon, Israel, Greece, and Rome all had similar values.

Standards for volume measurement were hard to find. They varied from the Greek and Roman amphora (the name of a jar for storing oil or wine) to various barrels and bottles used for wine. Champagne bottles form a series, doubling in size, with the names magnum, jeroboam, rehoboam, methuselah, and balthazar (after characters in the Old Testament).

Greek temples and tombs

In ancient Greece people believed in many gods. Each god possessed particular attributes, and worshippers approached those gods they thought most likely to answer their particular prayers.

Gods closely resembled humans and they lived in places known as sanctuaries, such as woodland groves, caves, or mountaintops, in which shrines were set up with altars where worshippers could leave offerings. Some sanctuaries provided healing, administered by priests, and many were the sites of games. The Olympic Games were held every four years in the sanctuary at Olympia. That sanctuary dates from about 1000 B.C.

Other sanctuaries had an oracle (a person through whom the god spoke) offering advice to visitors. The most famous oracle—at the shrine to Apollo at Delphi—was the Pythia. Beginning in 582 B.C., the Pythian Games were held in the third year of each Olympiad (the four-year period between Olympic Games). Most oracles occupied chambers below ground, but the Pythia sat on a tripod stool in a small, low room. The first shrine at Delphi was destroyed by fire in 548 B.C., but the need to house an oracle and provide accommodation for priests, other officials, and competing athletes meant that some shrines were enclosed in buildings.

Greek civilization arose from the Minoan civilization, founded by settlers from Anatolia (present-day Turkey) who colonized Cyprus, Crete, and some parts of Greece around 3000 B.C. The Minoans' principal god was female and depicted as a woman. After 2000 B.C. power became increasingly concentrated in the hands of the ruler of the city of Knossos in Crete. Not far from the palace at Knossos, built in about 1900 B.C., there is a temple containing a tomb, suggesting that by then the Minoan rulers themselves were worshipped as gods.

Curriculum Context

Students are expected to describe how technology has affected individuals, societies, and cultures.

A tholos was a circular shrine. This one, built at Delphi in about 390 B.C., originally had 20 huge pillars around the outside.

Building temples

When the Greeks began to represent their gods with large statues, the statues had to be protected from the weather. The buildings erected to house them were known as naoi, literally "dwellings." The image was placed in a central room called the cella, which was open at the eastern end. At first these temples were made from wood and mud brick, and the images were wooden; but as old structures decayed, they were rebuilt with stone and brick. The buildings were rectangular and built on an east–west axis with an entrance porch at one end covered with a roof supported by columns. Later temples had a porch at either end and were surrounded by columns. The first-known example of a temple surrounded by columns is the Temple of Hera (Heraion) at Samos, built in 750 B.C.

Curriculum Context

The curriculum requires a knowledge of the physical properties of construction materials.

Another temple of Hera, at Olympia, was built in about 600 B.C., originally with wooden columns, which were later replaced in stone. There were six columns at each end and 16 columns along each side. The cella contained statues of Hera, Zeus, and Hermes.

The Parthenon, built of white marble on the hill of the Acropolis at Athens, is the largest and most famous of all Greek temples. It was built under the supervision of the Greek sculptor Phidias. Work began in 447 B.C., and the building was completed in 438 B.C., although the exterior decoration was not finished until 432 B.C. The Parthenon was dedicated to Athena Parthenos (Athena the Virgin) and contained a massive statue of her.

In 146 B.C. Greece became part of the Roman Empire; and when Christianity became the official religion of Rome, various emperors sought to stamp out the pagan Greek religion. Theodosius I (347–395 A.D.) banned the Olympic Games in 394 A.D., but otherwise the imperial edicts had little effect. The Greeks held to their traditional beliefs. Little by little the Greeks converted, however, and their temples gradually became Christian churches. The Parthenon became a Byzantine church and then a Roman Catholic church. The Temple of Athena at Syracuse, Sicily, built between 474 and 460 B.C., was made into a Christian church in

Remembering the Dead

From the 6th century B.C. the Greeks began making stelae (carved slabs of stone) to commemorate the dead. The earliest ones showed a likeness of the deceased. Later stelae showed a scene from the dead person's life. The one here shows a woman with two doves, symbols of Aphrodite, the goddess of love and fertility. Greek statues and stelae were always painted, so originally this figure would have been brightly colored. Greek sculptors used metal tools to carve stelae from stone—often white marble or soft limestone quarried locally. Marble and limestone blocks were cut from the quarry face by hammering long, chisel-edged metal rods into natural joints in the rock. The blocks were then sawn into slabs.

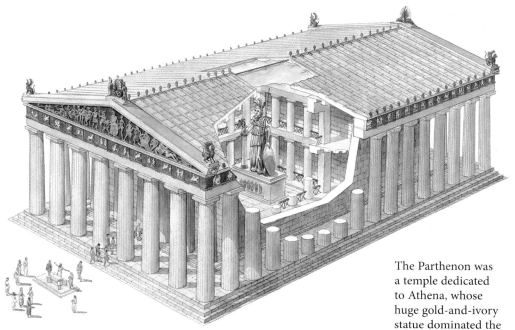

The Parthenon was a temple dedicated to Athena, whose huge gold-and-ivory statue dominated the interior.

640 A.D. and is now a cathedral. The Temple of Concord, built in the 5th century B.C. at what is now Agrigento, Sicily, became a church in 597 A.D.

Life after death

It was the Greek custom to cremate the dead and to keep the ashes in an urn. A grave found on the island of Évvoia contains the remains of a man and woman who died in about 1000 B.C. The man's ashes were placed in a large bronze urn, and various gold objects were buried with the woman. The presence of snaffle bits shows that horses were buried there as well. The grave was inside what had been an impressive building.

After death it was believed that everyone went to the House of Hades, god of the underworld. In life, however, people were not equal. Some were braver, stronger, wiser, or more generous than others. By the 8th century B.C. the Greeks believed that people with superior qualities might retain them in the underworld. This ensured them a privileged position after death and would allow them to continue to help the living. They became heroes, and shrines were erected to them.

Bronze

A hard durable alloy made of copper and tin.

Mesoamerican pyramids

Despite their apparent similarities, the pyramids of Egypt and those in central America are unrelated. The Mesoamerican pyramids were constructed thousands of years later. And rather than serving as private tombs for rulers, they were used mainly as public temples for purposes of ritual and celebration.

In about 30 A.D. in the Valley of Mexico the volcano Xitle erupted, burying the nearby city of Cuicuilco. It was not until 1922 that archaeologists discovered the ruins of the city and the lower part of its circular pyramid. The pyramid was built in four tiers, with a core made from clay and rubble faced with broken blocks of volcanic rock. Two ramps, on opposite sides of the pyramid, led to the temple that once stood on the top of the pyramid.

Cuicuilco is located on the southern side of modern Mexico City. It was at the peak of its splendor from about 600 to 200 B.C., when it was damaged by an earlier eruption of Xitle. Its pyramid was built during this period. Circular temples were usually dedicated to the Feathered Serpent god, which was known to many Mesoamerican peoples as Kukulkan and to the Aztecs as Quetzalcóatl. Kukulkan–Quetzalcóatl may have been the most important god to the people of Cuicuilco.

Mesoamerica

The region comprising the southern part of Mexico along with the countries of Central America.

The first pyramids

An earlier tradition of pyramid building had become widespread throughout Mesoamerica long before the time the Cuicuilco pyramid was built. The earliest pyramid known was built by the Olmec people near La Venta in the Mexican state of Tabasco some time around 900 B.C. The Olmec was the most prominent civilization during the Pre-Classic period of Mesoamerican culture from 1200 B.C. until 600 A.D. Olmec cities grew around a central mound on top of

which religious ceremonies were conducted. Pyramids replaced the mounds from about 900 B.C. There is no evidence of a ramp or stairway used to reach the top of the La Venta pyramid, so historians suspect it was more like a sculpture than a building, intended to represent the mountain that the Olmec believed reached to heaven and was the source of the corn (maize) on which agriculture depended.

One of the six large Mayan step pyramids at Tikal, Guatemala, each of which has a temple built on its summit.

The Maya, who followed the Olmec, also built pyramids, usually from stone blocks bonded with lime mortar and with steep stairways to the temple that only priests were permitted to climb. Tikal, Guatemala, is the largest and possibly oldest Mayan city. Occupied between about 800 B.C. and 900 A.D., at one time it was home to about 100,000 people. The city center contained palaces and other important buildings as well as a number of small pyramids and six very large pyramids, each with a temple at the top. Archaeologists have numbered the pyramids from I to VI in the order they were built. Pyramid I, topped by the Temple of the Jaguar, was built in 695 A.D. and Pyramid VI in 766 A.D. The tallest building is Pyramid IV, built in 720 A.D. It is approximately 230 feet (70 m) high, and its steps lead to the Temple of the Two-Headed Serpent. A chamber in the temple was designed to amplify the voice of the priest standing in it, so the people in the square below could hear him. A Mayan aristocrat was buried in the pyramid beneath the temple.

Shrines and tombs

Although prominent people were sometimes buried in them, Mesoamerican pyramids were not primarily tombs. They represented the three levels of the Universe: the subterranean, terrestrial, and celestial. In 1971 a cave was discovered beneath the center of one pyramid. A long passage led from the cave to a room shaped like a four-leaf clover. The room contained many objects that confirmed its use as a shrine. The shrine had probably existed for a long time before the pyramid was built over it.

The people who fled from Cuicuilco in about 30 A.D. settled in Teotihuacán, about 30 miles (50 km) northeast of modern Mexico City. The area had been inhabited since at least 400 B.C., and Teotihuacán was then a small town. The new arrivals stimulated a rapid urban expansion. At its peak in about 500 A.D. Teotihuacán covered approximately 8 square miles (21 sq. km), and its population of 125,000 to 200,000 made it one of the world's largest cities. Teotihuacán was destroyed by fire in about 750 A.D. When centuries later the Aztecs claimed what remained of it, they believed the city had been built by supernatural beings. We do not know the city's original name. Teotihuacán is its Aztec name, meaning Place of the Gods.

Curriculum Context

Students are expected to explain the factors that affect the quality of buildings, such as the availability of materials and workers.

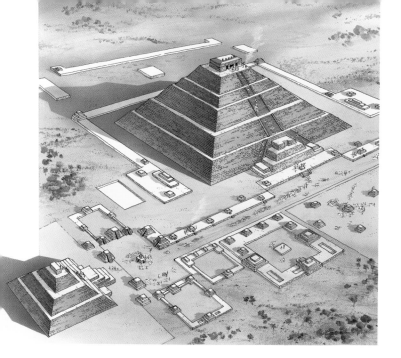

The Pyramid of the Sun in Teotihuacán as it would have appeared in its heyday. To the left is the smaller Pyramid of the Moon, where evidence of many sacrificial victims has been found.

The Place of the Gods

The 130-foot- (40-m-) wide Street of the Dead runs for 1.5 miles (2.4 km) through the center of the city of Teotihuacán. The Pyramid of the Moon, with platforms and smaller pyramids on either side, sits at the northern end of the street. This pyramid is 140 feet (43 m) tall and built with a solid core of rubble covered by a larger pyramid and with a third pyramid covering that. In 1998 archaeologists found burial pits with many rich burial goods deep inside the Pyramid of the Moon.

The Temple of the Feathered Serpent stands on top of another pyramid at the southern end of the street. It contained the remains of 18 men, apparently soldiers who had been ritually sacrificed.

The Pyramid of the Sun, standing on the eastern side of the street, is the biggest of all the pyramids, rising to 216 feet (66 m) and measuring about 720 by 760 feet (220 by 232 m) at its base. A cave beneath the pyramid was probably a shrine.

Gears, axles, cams, and cranks

Gears, axles, cams, and cranks are all types of simple machines that have been in use for over one thousand years, simplifying our lives in ways that we now take for granted, and laying the foundations for the more complex machines that we use today.

Curriculum Context

Students are expected to be able to calculate speed, momentum, acceleration, work, and power in systems such as in the human body.

The shadoof was originally developed in Mesopotamia, in around 2500 B.C. At one end of the lever hangs a bucket and at the other is a counterbalancing weight. The bucket scoops up water from a well or pond, and the lever then rotates to deposit the water elsewhere.

The human body is perhaps the greatest and most versatile machine ever developed. Our skeleton works like an elaborate collection of levers and pulleys that can lift heavy objects and move at different speeds with a grace and subtlety that defies even the most advanced robots. But there are limits to how fast we can run, how much we can lift, and how much work we can do before we tire. For all the wonder of the human body the development of modern society has relied very heavily on artificial machines, progressively improved through the ages, to replace muscle power and increase the strength and force available to us.

From hand tools to the first simple machines

Strictly speaking, a machine does not have to be a large and noisy contraption made of engines, gears, and wheels—it can be any device that converts a small force into a larger one. A spade is a simple machine because it converts a small force at the handle into a much larger force at the sharpened blade using what is known as the principle of the lever. Pulleys, screws, wedges, and ramps are other common examples of simple machines.

The earliest machines were little more than hand tools. Eyebrow tweezers (based on the lever) date from around 3500 B.C. in the ancient Sumerian civilization (in what is now Iraq). Most of the earliest agricultural tools also used the principle of the lever, including the shears (invented around 4500 B.C.) and the plow (in use by 3000 B.C.).

An image from *Les Très Riches Heures du Duc de Berry* (an early-15th century book of hours) showing the zodiac calendar for March. This was the time for sowing, and plows were drawn by oxen.

Agriculture has always relied on effective irrigation, and some of the first recognizable machines were devices for moving water from one place to another. The shadoof (also called the swape) enables a human operator to raise a heavy bucket of water several feet high using a long lever with a counterweight at one end. It is shown in reliefs produced by the Akkadian civilization (adjoining the Sumerian region) from around 2500 B.C. and has been used in Egypt since around 2000 B.C. More sophisticated water-raising machines include the rotating auger screw, which was thought to have been invented by the ancient Greek mathematician Archimedes (*c*.287–212 B.C.) in the third

Lever

A simple machine consisting of a rigid bar pivoted on a fixed point and used to transmit force.

century B.C. One version consists of a pipe leaning at an angle of 45 degrees with its lower end in water and a large screw wound around the inside. As the pipe is rotated, the screw lifts the water to the top, where it is collected. This ancient example of a water pump is still used today in many countries.

Greek inventors were the original mechanics; the word machine comes from the Greek word *mechane*, which translates loosely as device. The Greeks pioneered the use of mechanical dolls and toys called automata (giving us the word automatic). Although automata were trivial devices designed for amusement, their ingenious mechanisms inspired many later inventions.

Another important Greek inventor, Hero of Alexandria (*c.*62 A.D.), advanced the theory of the five simple machines—the lever, the wheel and axle, the pulley, the ramp, and the screw. He also developed numerous devices, including one for automatically opening the doors of a temple using hot air.

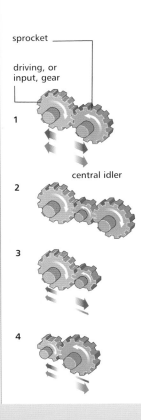

sprocket

driving, or input, gear

1

central idler

2

3

4

Different Kinds of Gears

A gear is a wheel with teeth (sprockets) cut into its outer edge that fits together (meshes) with a second, similar wheel. As they rotate, one wheel moves clockwise and one counterclockwise (1). If both wheels need to move in the same direction, a smaller wheel called a central idler can be placed between them (2).

Gears can be used either to change the speed of rotation or the torque (twisting power) of an engine. If both gear wheels have the same number of teeth, they turn at the same speed with equal power, or torque. If one wheel has twice as many teeth as the other, it turns at half the speed but with twice as much power. If the

larger wheel drives the smaller wheel (3), the speed is doubled and the power is halved, which means the mechanical advantage is ?. If the smaller wheel drives the larger wheel (4), the speed is halved and the power is doubled, so the mechanical advantage is 2.

In bicycles and automobiles gears are used in both of these ways. On the level the automobile transmission system works as a speed multiplier to make the wheels turn quicker than the engine. Traveling uphill, gears are used as power multipliers: although the wheels turn less quickly than the engine, the greater power that results is used to get the vehicle up the slope.

Water wheels convert the energy of flowing water into more useful forms of power. In this image, water turns the large wheel, which turns the smaller axle, allowing heavy material to be hoisted up easily from a mine.

Rotary motion

Potter's wheels were being used to make pottery as early as 3250 B.C. around the Turkish peninsula, although the potter's wheel was never taken up in pre-Columbian America. Wheels were not used for transportation until around 3,000 years later, when the wheel and axle were developed by the Sumerians.

Gear wheels probably date from ancient Greece. The philosopher and mathematician Aristotle (384–322 B.C.) recorded the use of gears without teeth, and the physicist and inventor Ctesibius of Alexandria (c.270 B.C.) developed a water clock using gears about 200 years later. Gears were an immensely important

Curriculum Context

The curriculum requires an awareness that technological advances can remain useful for long periods of time.

invention and developed in two different directions. Large wooden gears became essential components in machines for transforming rotational motion in different ways, such as in water mills and windmills. Much later, finely machined metal gears were used in clocks and scientific instruments. Gears were the electronic components of their day, used in precision chronometers (clocks used for navigation on board ships) invented by British watch- and clockmaker John Harrison (1693–1776), and in early mechanical computers developed by British mathematician Charles Babbage (1791–1871).

Powering machines

It was not until the Roman Empire (27 B.C. to A.D. 395) that machines started to make full use of rotating parts. This enabled the Romans to develop new ways of powering their machines using treadmills (almost like gigantic mouse wheels driven by humans) and water wheels. Partly due to the abundance of slaves in ancient Rome, treadmills were the most common form of machine power. They were used to power corn mills, olive presses, water-raising devices, and early cranes.

Curriculum Context

Students should be able to calculate power in systems such as machines.

Although horizontal water wheels were probably developed in ancient Greece, efficient, vertically mounted water wheels were described by the first-century Roman architect and engineer Vitruvius only in A.D. 27. The Vitruvian wheel was used to mill corn using crude wooden gears to drive heavy millstones. Later, water mills were used to power a variety of different machines. From the first century A.D. the Chinese were using water mills to make paper, and water-powered mechanical hammers were in use 200 years later. Water power spread rapidly toward the decline of the Roman Empire. By A.D. 1086, when the Domesday Book (a comprehensive survey of English landholdings) was completed, no fewer than 5,600 water mills had been built in England.

It is surprising that wind power made no appearance in Greek or Roman civilization, because sailing ships had been used in Egypt since at least 2500 B.C. Large-scale windmills probably date from around A.D. 600 in Persia (modern-day Iran), and they were not used in Europe until around 500 years later.

Mechanically transmitting and converting power
From the end of the Roman Empire until the Industrial Revolution in the 19th century, machines became more complex and more refined.

During the Middle Ages in Europe machines began to evolve into the complex collections of wheels, gears, and levers that are familiar today. The key to this development was an understanding of how to transform power from a single source in various ways, and particularly how to change rotational motion into reciprocating (up-and-down) motion. Two inventions were important here: the cam and the crank.

Curriculum Context

Students should be aware that in history, diverse cultures have contributed technological advances to various machines, such as wheels and axles.

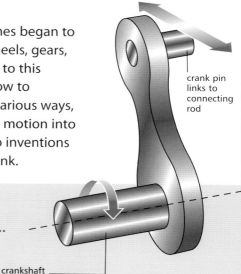

crank pin links to connecting rod

crankshaft

Cams and Cranks

The cam was first described in ancient Greece by Hero of Alexandria. It often takes the form of an egg-shaped wheel fastened to an axle on which one end of a rod rests. As the axle rotates, the egg-shaped cam raises and lowers the rod, thus converting the rotational motion of the axle into up-and-down motion in the rod. In automobile engines cams are often used to open and close the valves that let in air and fuel to the cylinders.

The crank was first used in ancient China around A.D. 100. It is effectively a handle bent out of the central axle of a wheel. A later modification, the crank and connecting rod, was developed in 1430. Adding a rod to the crank that connects it to

machinery allowed up-and-down motion to be converted into rotary motion, or vice versa. The crank can be used to convert the up-and-down motion of a piston in a steam engine, for example, into the rotary motion of wheels. In a modern four-stroke automobile engine a connecting rod links the pistons inside the cylinders to the crankshaft, which transmits (via the transmission) the up-and-down motion of the pistons to the rotating wheels that drive the vehicle forward or backward.

Archimedes' inventions

Archimedes is considered to be one of the greatest mathematicians of all time. His theorems and philosophies became known the world over, and his inventions brought him recognition and fame that lasts to this day.

Curriculum Context

Students should be able to research and describe the history of science and the contributions of scientists.

Archimedes (*c.*287–212 B.C.) was the greatest mathematician and physicist of the ancient world. He was born in Syracuse, Sicily (then a Greek colony), the son of an astronomer named Phydias. The family was friendly with Hieron II, the king of Syracuse, and even possibly related to him. Archimedes first studied in Alexandria, Egypt, where his teacher was a former pupil of Greek mathematician Euclid (fl. *c.*300 B.C.). His studies completed, he returned to Syracuse, where he remained for the rest of his life.

Innovator and inventor

Although he was not the first person to use levers, Archimedes was the first to work out the principle underlying them. He said that if he had somewhere to stand and a lever long and strong enough, he could move the world. This claim led King Hieron to even challenge Archimedes to move a very heavy object. Archimedes is said to have responded by assembling a system of levers and pulleys with which Hieron himself was able to pull the royal ship Syracusa—fully laden with passengers and freight—out of the dry dock, across land, and into the harbor.

Archimedes is said to have designed a planetarium and also the screw pump to help with irrigation of crops (although the Egyptians may have had this much earlier). It is a spiral screw inside a cylinder. When turned, it raises water, and it is still used today.

Planetarium

An apparatus or display representing the celestial bodies and other astronomical phenomena, and the building or room containing this apparatus.

With the aid of various machines devised by Archimedes, including the fearsome "claws," the city of Syracuse held out against the Roman siege for three years.

An Archimedes screw pump is angled so that the tip of the tube is in the water. With each turn of the handle, water rises over each thread of the screw until it flows out of the tube's upper end.

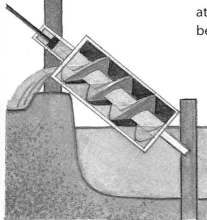

Fearsome weapons

Archimedes also invented weapons that are said to have struck terror into the hearts of the Romans when they laid siege to Syracuse in 215 B.C. Anticipating the Roman attack, the king decided to commission Archimedes to design a defensive system for the city. It involved rebuilding the walls to accommodate powerful catapults, cranes that lifted large boulders and dropped them onto the troops below, and also several novel weapons. His weapons held the invaders at bay for three years, turning the siege into a battle between the Romans and Archimedes.

The "claws of Archimedes" were among the most fearsome of his weapons. They would descend onto any ship that came within range, seize hold of the vessel, and shake it violently or even lift it high into the air and swing it about until all the soldiers were shaken out of it. The ship was then dropped onto the rocks. No one knows exactly how the claws worked, but probably the device was a large grappling hook lowered by a tall crane. The hook gripped the prow of a ship then rose, lifting the vessel by the bow out of the sea until it was almost upright before suddenly releasing it.

Legend also tells of a focusing mirror that worked as a burning glass. It was said that it set fire to the sails of any ship that approached close enough for its archers to be within range of the city wall, but it is far from certain that such a weapon existed.

His inventions made him famous and gave rise to many legends, but Archimedes seems to have thought his mechanical devices were unworthy of him, and he published only his mathematical work. Consequently, it is impossible to say whether he really built all the machines credited to him.

Archimedes' Principle

King Hieron of Syracuse had commissioned a new crown, specifying that it must be made from pure gold. But when it was delivered, he doubted its purity. He asked Archimedes to determine, without damaging the crown, whether the gold had been mixed with cheaper silver. Archimedes could think of no way of doing this until one day when he overfilled his bath. When he stepped into it, it overflowed. He realized that when an object is immersed in water it displaces its own volume of water, and its weight decreases by the weight of the displaced water. He was so excited that he is said to have run naked through the town shouting "Eureka!" ("I've got it!"). He measured the precise volume of the crown by immersing it in water, then borrowed a piece of gold weighing exactly the same as the crown and measured its volume the same way. Silver is less dense than gold and therefore bulkier, so when Archimedes found that the crown displaced more water than the same weight of pure gold, he was able to tell the king that the goldsmith had cheated him.

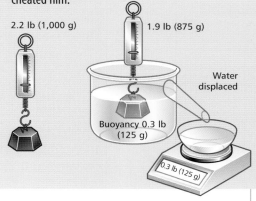

2.2 lb (1,000 g)   1.9 lb (875 g)

Water displaced

Buoyancy 0.3 lb (125 g)

0.3 lb (125 g)

Mathematics

Archimedes was primarily a mathematician. He calculated a value for π (pi) that is very close to the modern approximation, and devised methods for calculating the volume and surface area of a body with a curved surface—anticipating the integral calculus by 2,000 years. He found a way to express very large numbers, demonstrating it with a calculation of the number of grains of sand that exist in the Universe.

The Romans finally took Syracuse in about 212 B.C., and the general, Marcellus, ordered that Archimedes and his house should not be harmed. A Roman soldier found Archimedes working on a mathematical problem. When the soldier demanded that Archimedes accompany him, the mathematician told him not to disturb the circles he had drawn in the sand. Impatient, the soldier killed him.

Archimedes' principle can be demonstrated by immersing a heavy item in water. The water exerts an upward force (buoyancy) on the item, and the item's weight decreases. The water displaced by the item flows out of a spout into a bowl. The buoyancy is equal to the weight of the displaced water.

Indian Ganga River technology

Indian civilizations that developed along the valleys of the Ganga and Indus rivers were masters of the technologies involved in managing an erratic water supply and working with metals.

Pastoralists

People who primarily live by raising and herding livestock, such as cattle, sheep, and goats.

About 1500 B.C. Aryan people began migrating southwestward into the broad plain of the Ganga (formerly Ganges) River, in what is now northern India. There were many fierce battles in which Aryan tribes defeated the people already occupying the land, but the Aryans were primarily pastoralists and farmers. They settled in villages, tilled the land, and eventually established Indo-Aryan kingdoms, where the Brahman religion and the Sanskrit language developed. Dynasties rose and fell, boundaries shifted, and in about 321 B.C. Chandragupta Maurya became the first ruler of the Mauryan Dynasty. Chandragupta greatly expanded the empire.

Rice was the staple food of the people living on the Ganga Plain. Archaeologists have found charred rice

grains in Bihar in northeast India dating from 2000 to
1500 B.C. Rice also became the most important crop
grown by the Aryan farmers.

There are two ways to grow rice. On sloping ground in
the hills rice is grown as a field crop, watered by the
rain. In the lowlands it is raised in seedbeds then it is
transplanted into flooded fields called paddies, which
are drained before harvesting. Paddy rice produces
bigger yields than upland rice, but its successful
cultivation depends on careful management of the
water supply. Water management is especially
important in India's monsoon climate, where nearly
all the rain falls during the summer.

Canals and irrigation

Dams, artificial lakes, and irrigation systems were
being used during the reign of Chandragupta Maurya
(reigned 321–296 B.C.), and some of the irrigation
schemes used rainwater or floodwater that had been
harvested and stored. Inundation canals were widely
used in Bengal (also in northeast India). These broad,

Rice is grown in
paddy fields on the
Ganga Plain, where
water is diverted
from the river into
the fields using
irrigation canals.

Wootz Steel

Wootz steel—its name is derived from *ukku*, the Telugu word for steel—was being made in Andhra Pradesh in eastern India by the 3rd century B.C. A solid lump of hot iron with a spongy consistency was hammered to rid it of slag and other impurities, then broken into smaller pieces. They were mixed with chips of green wood and sealed in a clay container. The container was heated until the iron melted and absorbed carbon from the wood. This process converted the iron into steel with a carbon content of between 1 and 1.6 percent. Steel with such a high carbon content becomes brittle when it is cooled by quenching it in water, but the Indian workers discovered how to temper the metal by reheating it. The result was a steel suitable for making knife and sword blades that were both flexible and had a razor-sharp edge.

shallow canals were opened when meltwater from the mountains combined with the monsoon rains to raise river levels. Water rich in silt flowed along the canals and through openings in their sides into smaller channels leading to the fields. Once the river level began to fall, the main canals were closed.

Ahar-pyne was a similar system developed on sloping ground in Bihar. Pynes are channels leading from the river to an ahar, which is a rectangular basin enclosed by embankments on three sides, with the natural slope of the land forming the fourth.

A tank built in the 1st century B.C. at Sringaverapura near Allahabad in northern India is perhaps the most remarkable example of water harvesting. It is 800 feet (244 m) long, 60 feet (18 m) wide, and 12 feet (3.7 m) deep and lined with brick. Water from the Ganga River flowed downhill and through two deep earthen tanks, where silt settled to the bottom. Water left each of these tanks from outlets near the top; as it entered the main tank the water passed over steps between curved walls that slowed the flow. To make sure water was available in the dry season, several wells were dug in the bottom of the tank.

Curriculum Context

Students should understand the need to conserve water and water sources.

Metalworking

Indian technology continued to advance. In the grounds of the Quwwat-ul-Islam (Might of Islam) Mosque in the Mehrauli area of Delhi there stands a cast-iron pillar that is more than 23.5 feet (7 m) tall and 16 inches (40 cm) in diameter. It weighs more than 6.6 tons (6 tonnes). The iron pillar was erected in 415 A.D. during the classical period in Indian history that began with the founding of the Gupta Dynasty in 320 A.D. It was commissioned by Kumara Gupta (reigned 415–455 A.D.) in honor of his father Chandra Gupta II, and it is inscribed with accounts of Chandra's military exploits.

It was not until late in the 19th century that European ironworkers were capable of casting a single piece of metal the size of Kumara's iron pillar. The pillar possesses another remarkable feature: Despite having stood in the open for over 1,500 years, there is not a trace of rust on its surface. This is due partly to the dry climate—although it rains heavily during the summer monsoon—but also to impurities in the iron.

The iron pillar of Delhi has been exposed to all weather for over 1,500 years, but it shows no signs of rust due to its unusual metallurgy (metal technology).

Roman roads and aqueducts

From the 4th century B.C. the Romans built roads throughout their sprawling empire. To replace the earlier tracks that consisted of clinging mud in winter and choking dust in summer, they constructed well-engineered stone roadways built on solid foundations. Any water drained off their cambered surface into drains and ditches along the side of the road.

An extensivre infrastructure

At their peak Roman roads totaled over 50,000 miles (80,000 km) of highways—enough to stretch twice around the world. There were 29 great military roads spreading out from Rome. In addition, there was a system from Carthage in North Africa that ran along the southern coast of the Mediterranean Sea; in Gaul (France) roads radiated from Lyon; and in Britain London was the hub of the road system. The first Roman road was the Via Appia (Appian Way) built southward from Rome in 312 B.C. by Roman general Appius Claudius Caecus (fl. 4th century B.C.). At first it ran only as far as Capua but it was later extended to the coast at Brundisium (present-day Brindisi) in southern Italy. Other roads soon followed, such as the Via Aurelia to Genua (Genoa) and the Via Flaminia to the Adriatic coast, each named after a different Roman dignitary.

A layered structure gave Roman roads their stability, while the surface enabled rainwater to drain into ditches or gutters at either side.

curb stones

large surface stones

gravel

bank

ditch

foundation of stone slabs

Road construction

The Romans built roads mainly so that couriers, merchants, and administrators such as tax collectors could go about their business. But of course they were useful for moving troops rapidly in case of trouble with the local people. Wherever possible, the roads followed a straight line set out by surveyors using a sighting staff called a groma, and the roads tended to turn (if they had to) at high points where the viewing was easy. For a major highway the engineers first dug parallel drainage ditches about 40 feet (12 m) apart, then excavated a shallow trench between them, which they filled with sand, mortar, and a succession of stone courses to form the foundation of the road. They topped a watertight layer of crushed stone with a surface pavement of stone slabs or cobbles set in mortar. They made concrete from crushed stones, pozzolana (volcanic ash) cement if available, and lime. On marshy ground the whole road was raised above the surrounding countryside.

Primary roads, known as *viae*, were paved to keep the surface dry and free from mud. They were so well constructed that many still exist, such as this one in Timgad, Algeria. Some continue to be used even today.

Curriculum Context

Students should know that engineers often work in teams, with different individuals performing different tasks that contribute to the results.

Some of the major roads in Italy had stone curbs 8 inches (20 cm) high and 2 feet (60 cm) wide on each side, with side lanes outside them that operated as one-way streets. Drivers of fast two-wheeled chariots could achieve 75 miles (120 km) a day along these roads, with the eight-horse freight wagons covering a more modest 15 miles (25 km) a day. As the Roman Empire crumbled, so did its roads due to a lack of maintenance. Later road builders sometimes took over the Roman routes, as can still be seen by the arrow-straight stretches on any road map of England.

Aqueducts

As Roman towns and cities increased in size, there was an increasing demand for water for the people to drink and to wash in—public baths and fountains were features of many Roman towns. To bring in the water, Roman engineers built aqueducts. An aqueduct is any permanent channel for carrying water. It may be an

Curriculum Context

Students should be able to describe how and why technology evolves.

A remarkable feat of engineering, the three-tiered aqueduct known as the Pont du Gard was built over the Gard River to carry water to the French city of Nîmes.

open or closed culvert, a tunnel through a hill, or—at its most spectacular—a viaduct across a valley.

Between 312 B.C. and 200 A.D., engineers built 11 aqueducts just to take water into Rome, some from more than 56 miles (90 km) away. They constructed them with a gentle downward slope, and the water flowed along by gravity. Other Roman aqueducts in Italy, Greece, and Spain are still used today. The aqueduct at Segovia, Spain, for example, was authorized by Roman emperor Trajan (53–117). It is made from 24,000 granite blocks fitted together without mortar to form a 2,400-foot (730-m) series of 165 arches. The three-tiered arches of the famous Pont du Gard near Nîmes, France, extend for 900 feet (275 m) and reach a maximum height of 165 feet (50 m). It was built in about 20 B.C. by Roman general Marcus Agrippa (63–12 B.C.). Both of these examples are still in full working order.

Curriculum Context

Students should be able to identify the chemical, mechanical, and physical properties of engineering materials.

The Mayan civilization

Although they were not the earliest of the Mesoamerican civilizations, the Maya are usually considered to have been the most noteworthy. While much of Europe still slumbered in the "Dark Ages," these innovative people created awe-inspiring temples and pyramids, highly accurate calendars, and hieroglyphic writing.

Of all the civilizations of preconquest America, the Mayan was undoubtedly the greatest. The Maya developed a sophisticated writing system with about 850 hieroglyph characters. Some hieroglyphs represented ideas, and others stood for sounds. In many cases a picture of an object was used to represent the sound of its name when that sound occurred inside a word—a method known as "rebus writing." Mayan scholar-priests were also skilled astronomers and mathematicians. Their most remarkable achievement, however, was the Mayan calendar. Other American cultures used a similar calendar, but none developed it as well as the Maya.

Curriculum Context

The curriculum requires an awareness that science and technology have been practiced by people for a long time.

The first indications of the emerging Mayan civilization appeared between 300 B.C. and 100 A.D., a time historians call the Late Formative Period. During the Classic Period, between 250 and 900 A.D., the Maya erected many carved stone pillars, or stelae. That is when they were at their most influential and prosperous. That period ended in about 900 A.D. with the abandonment of the old ceremonial centers.

The Maya lived on the Yucatán Pensinsula of Mexico and Belize and the adjacent Petén limestone plateau of northern Guatemala, extending into parts of Honduras and El Salvador. The territory is mountainous and volcanic in the south, low-lying, hot, and wet in central Yucatán, and drier with thinner soils in the north.

Mayan carved pillars record the dates they were made, the names of the priests and nobles, and the most important events of the previous 20 years. The Maya also produced books, of which only three survive. The most important of them, called the Dresden Codex because it was acquired by the Saxon State Library in Dresden, Germany, contains astronomical tables.

Mayan astronomers accumulated a vast wealth of observations and used them to discern cycles in astronomical phenomena. For example, they were able to calculate that the Moon completes its cycle 149 times in 4,400 days. Therefore the time for one cycle— a lunar month—is 29.5302 days. The length accepted today is 29.53059 days.

The doors and windows of this ancient Mayan observatory are aligned to follow the orbit of Venus.

Astronomical tables

Records of information designed to enable the calculation of planetary positions, lunar phases, eclipses, and information for calendars.

Curriculum Context

Students should be aware that people have always invented techniques to solve problems.

The Maya could predict solar eclipses, though not the places where they would be visible. They were not aware that the Moon orbits Earth and Earth orbits the Sun, so their eclipse dates were based not on orbital calculations but on meticulous records. From their records they deduced that there is never a solar eclipse if the new Moon appears more than 18 days after the day when the Sun crosses the Moon's path. They calculated the average movements of Venus with an accuracy of one day in 6,000 years. They also realized that Venus is both the morning and evening star.

Numbers

In order to record dates and perform calculations, the Maya needed a number system; and in developing it they introduced two extremely important concepts: place values and a symbol for zero. A dot represented one, a horizontal dash five, and a picture of a shell represented zero. They were already using this notation by about 400 B.C.

Place values allowed them to write very large numbers clearly and conveniently. For example, in modern notation the number 276 is (2 x 100) + (7 x 10) + (6 x 1). The Maya counted to base 20 (we use base 10). This should give place values for 1, 20, 200, and so on, but the Maya gave them to 1, 20, then 18 x 20. This complicated their calculations, but 18 x 20 equals 360, which is the number of days that exist in the Mayan calendar.

The Mayan calendar

The Mayan calendar is their most famous creation. In fact, there were three calendars. The first was based on a sacred year of 260 days arranged in two overlapping cycles, the first comprising the numbers 1 to 13. The second was made up of 20 day names, which were also the names of gods. A number and the name of a god uniquely identified each day in the sacred year. But the sacred calendar was of no use to farmers. For everyday use there was a calendar based on a solar year. It was divided into 18 months each of 20 days plus five unlucky days—a "period with no name." People believed that someone who was born at that time was cursed for life.

The third calendar, used for "long counts," consisted of a series of cycles in which 20 kins (days) made 1 uinal; 18 uinals made 1 tun (360 days); 20 tuns made 1 katun (7,200 days); and 20 katuns made 1 baktun (144,000 days). The longest cycle was the alautun, of 23,040,000,000 days. For reasons that are not clear, the calendar counted from a zero date on August 13, 3114 B.C. For example, the date 8/11/15/3/18 means 8 baktuns, 11 katuns, 15 tuns, 3 uinals, and 18 kins have passed since date zero, giving the date July 9, 273 A.D.

Mayan scholars used a supplementary series of tables containing information about the lunar month and a secondary series based on a formula for correcting calendar dates to bring them into line with the lunar month and solar year. They also had to take account of sacrificial cycles of 4, 9, and 819 days, which were of religious importance.

Curriculum Context

Students should understand the need for units of measurement, such as for time, distance, weight, and volume.

This diagram shows how the sacred 260-day calendar worked. The wheel seen on the right has 13 numbers. The wheel on the left has 20 named days, each with a unique symbol. The wheels turn so that each number fits in with a day. After 13 days the right-hand wheel comes around to the first number again to begin a new week, this time starting on a different named day. The whole cycle took 260 days.

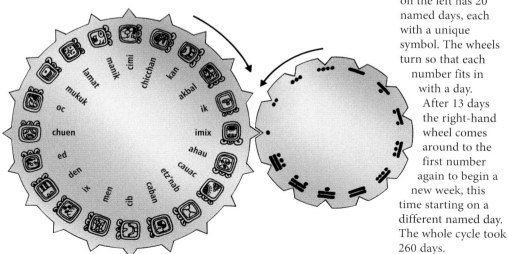

Ancient artillery

To provide backup for their foot soldiers and charioteers, the armies of ancient Greece and Rome used a range of heavy weapons to hurl rocks and arrows at the enemy. Many were built as defensive weapons, although some were mounted on wheels and deployed on the battlefield.

Greek weapons

The Greeks invented many of the early artillery weapons, which were later adopted and improved by Roman military engineers. The principal missile-throwing devices were catapults.

A Roman ballista from c.25 B.C. To load the ballista, the slider was pushed forward until the trigger engaged the string, and then the slider was wound back by the lever.

In 399 B.C. Dionysius the Elder (c.431–367 B.C.), ruler of the Greek colony at Syracuse on the island of Sicily, financed a research program to find new weapons for his forthcoming war with the Carthaginians. His engineers built an arrow-firing catapult that looked like a giant crossbow. They made the bow—about 7.5 feet (2.3 m) across—from strips of wood or horn laminated together (a so-called composite bow). To pull back the bow string, the firing team used a built-in winch that wound back a claw-and-trigger mechanism together with a grooved slider that was held in place by a ratchet. The groove held a 6-foot (2-m) arrow that was fired by moving the trigger to release the claw. A pivot near the front of the bow allowed the firers to aim the catapult in any direction. The Greeks even made a repeating version of the catapult called a

rope springs

arm

string

slider

trigger

lever

ratchet

polybolos ("multishooter"), which fired one arrow after another from a hopper or magazine that was mounted above the slider.

Two Roman soldiers set up a catapult to fire, by winching back the arm that holds stone ammunition.

Roman and Greek catapults

The Roman name for a catapult was *ballista*. They adapted the Greek design to fire 27-inch (69-cm) bolts and often mounted it on a wheeled iron frame. The Roman commander Vespasian (9–79 A.D.) used ballistas to great effect in his actions against Celtic warriors in Britain. Human remains dating from 43 A.D. that were discovered at the hill fort called Maiden Castle in southern England include a skull drilled right through with a ballista-bolt hole.

A slightly different Greek catapult design used twisted ropes rather than a bow as the motive power. Two skeins of twisted rope or animal sinews mounted

Curriculum Context

The curriculum requires an understanding that the position and motion of objects can be changed by pushing or pulling.

Roman soldiers attack a Greek fortress using slingshots and arrows.

vertically gripped the ends of two short lengths of wood. A drawstring joined the outer ends of these wooden "arms," rather like the bow string of a bow. When the firer winched back the string, the arms twisted the ropes even more. They untwisted with explosive force when the firer pressed a trigger to release the drawstring. One such catapult built for the Macedonian king Philip II (reigned 359–336 B.C.) fired spearlike arrows 13 feet (4 m) long; and Philip's son Alexander the Great (356–323 B.C.) employed similar weapons in his wars against the Persians.

Larger versions of this type of catapult hurled rocks instead of arrows. The Greek mathematician and engineer Archimedes (c.287–212 B.C.) is said to have constructed a catapult capable of throwing a rock weighing 175 pounds (79 kg) a distance of 200 yards (183 m). The huge machine was mounted on a ship for use against the attacking Roman fleet during the siege of Syracuse (215 B.C.). Even larger catapults were used on land, and with stones weighing up to 350 pounds (159 kg) hurled at them, brick-built city walls had to be made at least 15 feet (4.6 m) thick to withstand an assault by giant catapults.

Ancient Greek Siege Machines

The sambuca (siege ladder) was designed by the ancient Greek Damis of Colophon. Soldiers climbed a ladder to enter the top compartment. Stones and rocks were loaded into boxes at the rear, raising the men at the front to the level of the battlements. Fire-raisers were long wooden beams that carried caldrons of lighted coals, sulfur, and pitch, which were used to start fires in the enemy's stockade. The wooden beam was hollow with a central iron tube and one iron-clad end to prevent it catching fire. A soldier pumped bellows at the other end to keep the fire alight. Battering rams were used to shake down a section of a wall. The one shown here was used in the fourth century B.C. The ram is metal plated at the battering end and housed in a so-called tortoise shell made of fire-resistant compressed seaweed and ox-hide. The ram was pushed forward on its wheels with considerable force, then pulled back by ropes and pulleys.

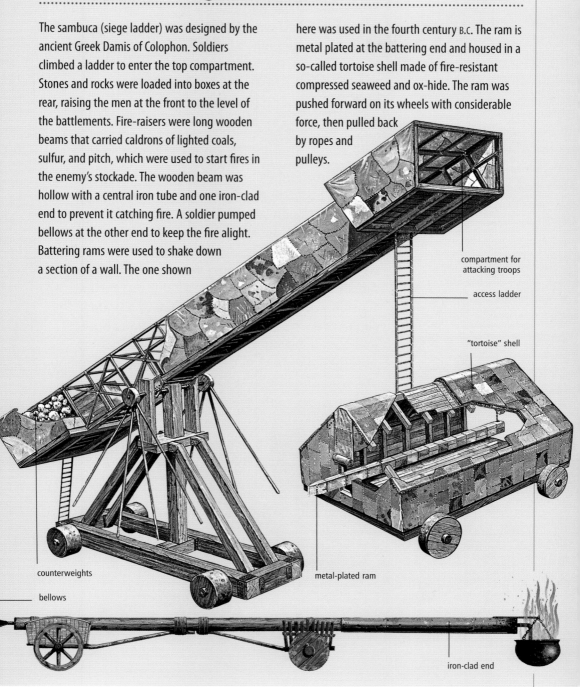

compartment for attacking troops

access ladder

"tortoise" shell

counterweights

bellows

metal-plated ram

iron-clad end

The onager

The slingshot is a very ancient hand weapon, used effectively by David to slay the giant Goliath, according to the Bible. In a slingshot a leather pouch at the end of a pair of strings holds a stone. The user hurls the stone at arm's length from behind his back or after twirling it around his head. The Romans mechanized this principle with a catapult they called the onager. (An onager is a wild ass that is infamous for kicking out with both back feet.)

It had a horizontal frame with two side beams that curved upward in the middle. A thick twisted sinew rope ran through large holes at the center of the beams and was anchored to the outside of each beam. The rope gripped one end of a long wooden arm that had iron hooks at the upper end to hold the sling. The firers used a winch to wind down the arm against the tension in the twisted rope, and placed a stone in the sling. When the arm was released, it sprang forward and hurled the stone. A large straw-filled cushion absorbed the shock of the arm at the end of its swing after the missile left the catapult.

Curriculum Context

Students should be aware that objects change their motion only when a net force is applied.

A Roman onager from *c.*350. The trigger bar was struck by a hammer to ensure a clean release. It was known as an onager, or "wild ass," because of its heavy recoil kick.

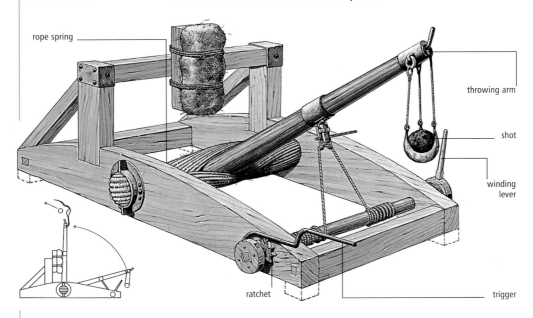

rope spring

throwing arm

shot

winding lever

ratchet

trigger

Greek Fire

A moving ship was a difficult target for a catapult, especially if the catapult itself was mounted on a ship. Even if the shot hit its target, it was unlikely to deal a mortal blow to the sturdily built hull of a Greek or Roman vessel. But these same ships—with their cloth sails and wooden hulls often coated with tar—burned easily. During the defense of Syracuse, Archimedes (*c*.287–212 B.C.) is said to have used a giant curved mirror to concentrate the Sun's rays on attacking Roman ships and set fire to them. In the early 670s Greek architect and chemist Callinicus, who was born in Syria in about 620 A.D., invented a flammable mixture that became known as "Greek fire."

Its exact composition is unknown, but it probably contained tar, resin, saltpeter, and sulfur. It may also have included mineral oil (petroleum). Enemy ships were bombarded with containers of the burning mixture, which continued to burn on the surface of the water even if the missiles did not make a direct hit. The mixture quickly set fire to ships' hulls and to any unfortunate sailors who jumped into the sea for safety. In 674 the defenders of Byzantium (present-day Istanbul) destroyed an attacking Arab fleet from Damascus using Greek fire. The Byzantines also used pumps as a kind of primitive flamethrower to squirt the burning mixture.

As with other catapults, onagers could be made on a very large scale. For example, there is a description of one that needed eight men on the winch to wind down the arm. But instead of having two vertical twisted rope springs and two horizontal arms (an arrangement that had to be carefully balanced), the onager had just one horizontal rope spring and a single vertical arm, and was therefore much easier to construct.

Technology advances

After the decline of the Roman Empire, armies in Europe continued to use catapults right through the Middle Ages. They developed the trebuchet, which was a lever system and worked a little like a seesaw. A rock on one end of a pivoted beam was hurled into the air by the action of a larger rock that made the other end of the beam fall. But eventually all types of catapults were superseded by the introduction of the cannon in the 14th century.

Timelines Prehistory—6000 B.C.

Technology

2,000,000 B.C. In Africa human ancestors (*Homo habilis*) make simple tools from pebblestones. One million years later *Homo erectus* begins chipping flakes off stones to sharpen them.

1,000,000 B.C. Human ancestors (*Homo erectus*) use hammers made from antlers to create tools for cutting, drilling, shaping, and hammering.

750,000 B.C. Fire is used by human ancestors (*Homo erectus*) in France.

500,000 B.C. Human ancestors (archaic *Homo sapiens*) in Europe use wooden spears with fire-hardened points. Three 400,000-year-old examples have been found in Germany.

250,000 B.C. Archaic *Homo sapiens* in Africa, Asia, and Europe use stone axes. 100,000 years later European toolmakers make knives by inserting a row of sharp flints into a grooved piece of wood or bone.

80,000 B.C. Stone lamps that burn oil or animal fat are used in Mesopotamia and western Europe.

45,000 B.C. Stone-headed spears are used in Europe. Flint knives are made in present-day Bulgaria.

38,000 B.C. African people go fishing with hooks and lines.

30,000 B.C. The tally stick (for counting, usually made of bone) is used in Africa and Europe. People make beads out of antler, bone, ivory, and seashells.

25,000 B.C. People in central Europe make ceramic images by firing clay models (they do not make pots).

20,000 B.C. The boomerang (made from mammoth tusk) is invented in northern Europe. The wooden bow and arrow are used in Spain and Saharan Africa. People in southern Europe use sewing needles made from bone.

Science

11,000 B.C. At about this time hunter-gatherers in northern Syria, east of Aleppo, cultivate rye.

10,000 B.C. Dogs are domesticated in Mesopotamia (present-day Iraq), probably first as food and later as pets and to help keep down rats. Centuries later, after goats and sheep are domesticated, dogs help protect flocks from wolves.

9000 B.C. Einkorn wheat is cultivated in Palestine. Previously people gathered the seeds of wild grasses. Einkorn (German meaning "one grain") provides larger grain; later (about 6000 B.C.) it is joined by the smaller emmer wheat, first cultivated in the area occupied by present-day Turkey.

8000 B.C. People in East Africa and Mesopotamia (present-day Iraq) domesticate goats and sheep. The animals provide milk and wool as well as meat. They also produce fat (tallow), with which people make rushlights and candles.

8000 B.C. In Central America pumpkins and squashes are domesticated, probably the first fruits cultivated for food, although indigenous people had been using the dried wild gourd calabash for making pots and bowls for a long time.

8000 B.C. The woolly mammoth (genus *Mammuthus*) becomes extinct, possibly because of climate change or because of overhunting by humans for food. Scientists have found complete specimens frozen in the permafrost of Siberia.

20,000 B.C. Cro-Magnon people in France produce stone blades shaped like leaves.

15,000 B.C. In Africa and, 2,000 years later, in southern Europe bone harpoons (barbed spears) are used for fishing.

13,000 B.C. By this time people add spear-throwers to their armory of weapons for hunting game and fish.

11,000 B.C. Mediterranean people fish using nets.

11,000 B.C. The earliest-known clay pots are made in Japan.

10,000 B.C. People in Palestine make houses of sun-dried bricks and also weave baskets.

8500 B.C. Indigenous people in North America make stone arrowheads.

7500 B.C. Clay tokens are used for record keeping in Mesopotamia.

6300 B.C. The earliest surviving dugout boat (hollowed from a tree trunk), found in the Netherlands, dates from this time.

6000 B.C. In northern Scandinavia wooden sleds are used to carry goods and to travel over snow. Cave paintings suggest that 1,000 years later people there may have begun using primitive skis.

6000 B.C. Palestinian people start using mortar to bind together sun-dried bricks for construction.

6000 B.C. Clay pottery is produced by people in Asia Minor (present-day Turkey). At about this time they also begin to weave cloth and make rope.

6000 B.C. The oldest-known pottery found to date in the Americas is produced by people who live in Santarém on the Amazon River basin in present-day Brazil.

8000 B.C. Barley is first grown and harvested as a crop by people in the Fertile Crescent in the Middle East.

7500 B.C. People in South America in the region of Peru domesticate chilies.

7000 B.C. Pigs in Asia Minor (in present-day Turkey) are domesticated for their meat, skin (which is made into leather), and bristles (made into brushes). About 2,000 years later people in southeast Asia independently domesticate pigs.

6500 B.C. People in Anatolia (in present-day Turkey) cultivate durum wheat, a variety rich in gluten that later Mediterranean people grind into flour for making pasta.

6500 B.C. At about this time people in Indonesia grow bananas, coconuts, and yams, while in neighboring New Guinea cultivation of sugarcane begins.

6500 B.C. Rice is grown in China in the delta of the Yangtze River, although the Hoabinhian people of southern China had gathered wild rice centuries earlier.

6500 B.C. Cattle are domesticated in Africa and Asia.

6500 B.C. People in Africa and the Middle East brew beer using wheat or barley.

6000 B.C. People in southwestern Asia cultivate flax to get fibers for making cloth.

6000 B.C. Farmers in the Middle East in the region of the Fertile Crescent begin to grow emmer wheat in preference to einkorn wheat.

Technology

5500 B.C. People in Anatolia (present-day Turkey) construct buildings using sun-dried bricks.

5200 B.C. Ancient Egyptians in the lower valley of the Nile River finally begin to practice settled agriculture, much later than other Middle Eastern peoples.

5000 B.C. Permanent villages begin to spring up in Central America, following the development of corn (maize) as a crop.

5000 B.C. In Mesopotamia (present-day Iraq) the distaff is used for spinning yarn from wool. The rod-shaped distaff holds combed wool, from which the spinster pulls fibers and twists them onto a spindle.

5000 B.C. The beam balance is invented in Egypt.

5000 B.C. People in Italy and the Middle East make mirrors out of the mineral obsidian, probably obtained from the island of Melos.

5000 B.C. Farmers living near the mouth of the Euphrates River in southern Mesopotamia (present-day Iraq) make houses of reeds lashed together and construct reed boats for use on the river.

5000 B.C. Copper is smelted in Egypt from ores dug out of the ground. Craftsmen use it to make weapons and other implements.

4400 B.C. Egyptians weave cloth on a loom, usually linen made from wild flax, which grows along the banks of the Nile River. (The Egyptians did not use wool.)

4300 B.C. People living near present-day Paris, France, make canoes from oak. The largest so far found is almost 16 feet (5 m) long.

4000 B.C. The brick-built arch is used in construction in Egypt and Mesopotamia.

4000 B.C. Egyptian craftsmen use flint saws for cutting wood and stone.

Science

5500 B.C. In Asia lentils and domesticated wheat (for breadmaking) are grown in the southwestern part of the continent; in Indochina from Burma (Myanmar) to Vietnam citrus fruits such as oranges and lemons become a commonly cultivated crop.

5500 B.C. The jungle fowl is domesticated in Southeast Asia. The red jungle fowl of India (domesticated c.2500 B.C.) is the ancestor of today's chicken.

5200 B.C. People in northern Iran make wine from the wild grapes that grow in the region. The fermentation process relies on yeasts that naturally form part of the white bloom on the ripe grapes.

5000 B.C. Farmers in northern Africa and Ethiopia grow various types of millet, including finger millet and bulrush millet, as the principal grain crop. So-called foxtail millet is preferred in central China.

5000 B.C. Arable farming begins in Mexico and other parts of Central America, with the people growing an early type of corn (maize) and other crops.

5000 B.C. People in India begin to cultivate date palms.

5000 B.C. People in settlements in the Middle East use cats for catching rats and mice.

5000 B.C. People in China grow peaches.

4000 B.C. In the Near East the process of distillation is practiced to make alcohol from wine for medicinal use.

4000 B.C. The lock (for doors) is invented in Mesopotamia (present-day Iraq). People there employ a harness to use oxen as draft animals.

4000 B.C. Egyptian boat builders make boat hulls by joining planks of wood together, rather than the reed boats and one-piece dugout canoes made previously. The new technique allows them to make larger wooden-hulled vessels.

3500 B.C. River barges with sails are used in Mesopotamia and Egypt.

3500 B.C. Farmers in Mesopotamia and China use a primitive plow.

3500 B.C. The wheel is invented in Mesopotamia, first as a hand-operated potter's wheel. At about this time people there start making bricks by firing clay in kilns, but use them only for special buildings.

3500 B.C. The Egyptians use a simple shadow clock, or gnomon—a vertical stick or obelisk that casts a shadow.

3200 B.C. The copper–tin alloy bronze is first used in Mesopotamia (present-day Iraq). The use of bronze spreads throughout the Middle East and Europe. By 2500 B.C. the Sumerians cast ax heads out of copper and bronze.

3200 B.C. Wheeled vehicles with axles are used in the Near and Middle East.

3100 B.C. The first stage of construction of Stonehenge—an earth bank with a ring of holes—begins in southern England.

3000 B.C. An industry making marble sculptures for export develops on the Greek islands in the Aegean Sea (the Cyclades).

3000 B.C. Copper ore deposits are discovered on the island of Cyprus in the Mediterranean Sea, and the island soon becomes the major source of the metal in the ancient world.

4500 B.C. In Central America avocados are grown, and cotton is cultivated.

4236 B.C. Ancient Egyptians introduce a 365-day calendar (12 months of 30 days plus a five-day holiday). This is the first precisely dated calendar; the next is the Sumerian calendar of about 3000 B.C.

4000 B.C. Domestication of horses occurs in the Ukraine.

4000 B.C. In parts of China the water buffalo is domesticated.

4000 B.C. Potatoes are cultivated as a food crop in the Andes Mountains of Peru.

4000 B.C. People in present-day Turkestan domesticate wild grapes and grow them to make wine.

4000 B.C. In Egypt the donkey is domesticated as a beast of burden.

3400 B.C. The Egyptians adopt numerals for quantities greater than 10 (with base 10).

3400 B.C. The Sumerians use a simple form of picture writing. By c.2400 B.C. it develops into cuneiform writing.

3200 B.C. The Egyptians measure the annual Nile flood. They estimate how much water is available for each farmer and how many crops he can grow.

3100 B.C. Egyptian scribes begin using hieroglyphs as a form of writing.

Technology

3000 B.C. To create an artificial lake for water for irrigation, Egyptian engineers build a 328-foot (100-m) dam across the Garawi River valley.

3000 B.C. Chinese and Egyptian sailors equip their boats with anchors.

3000 B.C. The earliest pottery in the Americas is made in Ecuador and Colombia.

3000 B.C. People in North America create rock shelters; they also produce items made of feathers, including blankets and baskets.

2800 B.C. The Sumerians make soap by boiling together animal fat and plant ashes.

2800 B.C. The Egyptians make papyrus (a kind of paper) out of crushed reeds. Previously, scribes wrote on parchment or vellum (very thin leather).

2750 B.C. Buildings with corbeled arches are constructed in Mesopotamia. The arch is made from overlapping pieces of stone, each one projecting farther than the one below. The same type of construction is also used to make stone domes.

2700 B.C. In China silkworms are cultured and fed on mulberry leaves. Strands of silk are unwound from their cocoons, made into fine yarn, and woven into silken cloth.

2630 B.C. Work begins on the stepped pyramid of Djoser at Saqqara in Egypt. Its base measures 345 feet (105 m) by 410 feet (125 m), and it is 203 feet (62 m) tall.

2600 B.C. People in Mesopotamia make glass by melting together sand (silica) and soda (sodium carbonate). At first it is used to produce glazes on pots and vases; later they learn to shape molten glass and make bottles.

2600 B.C. Egyptian builders use a set square for setting out right angles and a plumbline for checking verticals. Priests begin the practice of embalming dead dignitaries such as pharaohs to create mummies.

Science

3000 B.C. The Sumerians introduce a 360-day solar calendar with 12 months of 30 days. They add an extra month roughly every eight years to keep in step with the seasons.

3000 B.C. People establish towns in the Aegean region around Greece, based on the cultivation of olives and grapes.

3000 B.C. In West Africa yams are cultivated; palm trees are also grown for producing oil.

3000 B.C. People in Peru domesticate the llama.

2950 B.C. In China a lunar calendar is developed.

2900 B.C. Cotton is cultivated by people in the valley of the Indus River, India. It is spun into yarn to weave cloth.

2500 B.C. In Peru the peanut is domesticated as a food crop.

2500 B.C. People in northern Iran and northern Afghanistan domesticate the two-humped Bactrian camel.

2500 B.C. Tibetans domesticate the yak, a type of cattle with a long, shaggy coat.

2550 B.C. After 25 years' work the Great Pyramid of King Khufu (Cheops in Greek) is completed at Giza in Egypt. It is 482 feet (147 m) tall and measures 755 feet (230 m) across at the base. The granite stones weigh up to 15 tons (14 tonnes) each.

2500 B.C. Scandinavian people use wooden snowshoes.

2500 B.C. Clay water pipes are used for drains at Knossos in Crete and Mohenjo-Daro in Pakistan.

2500 B.C. The oldest-known Egyptian houses are built at Kahun.

2500 B.C. Sumerians in the city of Ur invent a process for soldering sheets of gold together.

2500 B.C. Tin ore is mined and smelted in Göltepe (in present-day Turkey). It becomes a source of the metal for alloying with copper to make bronze.

2490 B.C. Egyptian workmen build the mortuary temple of Pharaoh Menkaure, the smallest of the three pyramids at Giza.

2400 B.C. The parasol/umbrella is invented in Mesopotamia.

2400 B.C. People in Mesopotamia use bitumen, a tar that seeps from the ground near deposits of petroleum, for waterproofing buildings and boats. They also mix it with sand to make mastic as a building material.

2300 B.C. The Egyptians make wine from cultivated grapes. To improve (or disguise) the taste, they add terpentine-like resin. It produces a wine that probably tastes like modern retsina from Greece and Cyprus.

2300 B.C. The earliest known map, of Gasur at Nuzi (present-day Yorghan Tepe in Iraq), is produced on a clay tablet. It shows an area of land, probably a nobleman's estate.

2500 B.C. People in the valley of the Indus River domesticate the Indian elephant as a beast of burden.

2500 B.C. Sumerian traders introduce a system of standard weights, including the shekel and the mina.

2500 B.C. Egyptian physicians begin practicing surgery and develop a range of surgical instruments for the purpose.

2500 B.C. Chinese scientists practice acupuncture for healing ailments. Patients have tiny metal needles inserted at particular points on the body relating to the organ or organs that are sick.

2500 B.C. People in southeast Asia cultivate plots of breadfruit trees.

2400 B.C. The Egyptians domesticate cats, probably servals. Some cats are regarded as sacred and made into mummies

2300 B.C. Astronomers in Babylon study comets and observe the constellations.

2300 B.C. People in the Middle East keep geese. They collect and eat the eggs.

Technology

2300 B.C. King Sargon I of Akkad (reigned c.2334–2279 B.C.) produces maps of his kingdom in Mesopotamia for calculating the amounts of land taxes owed to him.

2300 B.C. Work begins on the main part of Stonehenge, a circle of huge standing stones on Salisbury Plain, England.

2200 B.C. An iron dagger blade dating from this time, found at Alaca Hüyük in Anatolia (modern Turkey), proves that iron is used for objects other than ornaments.

2100 B.C. The Sumerians construct a ziggurat (temple) near Ur, built out of sun-dried mud bricks.

2000 B.C. Women in Mesopotamia begin making perfume.

2000 B.C. Egyptian military engineers develop a portable battering ram.

2000 B.C. The Egyptians make metal mirrors from polished bronze.

2000 B.C. Spoked wheels rotating on the axle are used (on chariots) in Egypt and Mesopotamia, and bridles are used on horses.

2000 B.C. Egyptian craftsmen use a bow-drill for boring holes in stone.

2000 B.C. Copper is mined in the Great Lakes region of North America.

1950 B.C. Farmers in Palestine make plows with iron plowshares.

1600 B.C. Bellows are used in metalworking and glassmaking in Mediterranean countries.

1550 B.C. Farmers in southeastern Asia make plowshares with bronze.

1500 B.C. The Egyptians invent the shadoof—a bucket counterbalanced on a lever—for raising water from a well, a ditch, or a river.

1500 B.C. Egyptian workmen use metal files made of bronze for shaping objects.

Science

2000 B.C. Mathematicians in Babylon introduce a positional number system (in which the value of a digit depends on its position in a number) using base 60.

2000 B.C. People in Peru domesticate the guinea pig as a source of food.

2000 B.C. In Syria and Babylon medicine (based largely on astrology) becomes an important science. Recipes for ointments and poultices are recorded on clay tablets.

2000 B.C. Chinese emperors keep wild animals in captivity and establish one of the first zoos, called the Park of Intelligence.

1900 B.C. Farmers in Persia (now Iran) cultivate alfalfa (lucerne), probably as a fodder crop for feeding domestic animals such as cattle, sheep, and goats.

1800 B.C. Mathematicians in Mesopotamia discover what is now called Pythagorean theorem (concerning the lengths of the sides of a right-angled triangle).

1750 B.C. King Hammurabi of Babylon authorizes astronomers to compile catalogs of stars and planets.

1700 B.C. People in Syria develop an alphabet of about 30 symbols, each representing a different sound.

1650 B.C. Egyptian mathematicians learn how to solve simple equations, as indicated in the Rhind Papyrus, which was written at about this time. It was named for 19th-century Scottish Egyptologist Alexander Henry Rhind (1833–63), who collected it in 1858.

1500 B.C. The Olmec culture arises on the Gulf Coast plain of Central America, where its people begin building complexes of pyramids and temples.

1500 B.C. Wheeled toys are made by people in Mexico.

1500 B.C. The Mitanni people in Armenia (in western Asia) learn how to smelt iron from its ore, a technique picked up by the Hittites who conquered them in 1370 B.C.

1500 B.C. Egyptian engineers in Syria dam the Orontes River Valley to create a 19-square-mile (50-sq.-km) lake.

1500 B.C. People in the Aegean, around Greece, invent the beam press, which uses a weighted lever to squeeze juice from grapes for winemaking or oil from olives.

1500 B.C. Specialists in Egypt set up as professional millers, grinding cereals for a living (previously people made their own flour as they needed it).

1450 B.C. The Egyptians make a water clock (clepsydra) consisting of a vessel with a hole in the bottom. It measures time by the rate at which water flows out of the hole.

1450 B.C. For carrying huge stone obelisks along the Nile River, Egyptian craftsmen build barges up to 200 feet (61 m) long—the largest vessels so far constructed.

1450 B.C. Mesopotamian farmers use a single-tube seed drill, in which grain seeds from a funnel trickle down a tube into a groove plowed in the soil.

c.1400 B.C. The final stage of construction of Stonehenge is completed in southern England.

1350 B.C. Egyptian workmen weld iron at about the same time as the Hittites begin working with iron. Ironworking spreads to India by 1200 B.C. and Europe by 1000 B.C.

1600 B.C. Astrologers in Babylon recognize the zodiac, the path that the Sun, Moon, and planets (except Pluto) appear to take as they move across the sky.

1600 B.C. Olives are cultivated on the island of Crete in the Mediterranean Sea. People crush the fruit (including the stone) to make olive oil, which is exported.

1550 B.C. A papyrus known as the Ebers Papyrus—named for 19th-century German Egyptologist Georg Ebers (1837–98)—describes Egyptian medical practices and gives details of 700 drugs and other medications.

1500 B.C. Chinese people make beer. Also people in various parts of Asia produce alcohol (for drinking) by distilling wine.

1450 B.C. People in Manchuria, China, cultivate soybeans. They eat the beans fresh or dry them and store them for use in the winter. They also let them germinate and eat the bean sprouts or allow them to ferment and make them into soy.

1400 B.C. South American farmers grow cassava (manioc).

1361 B.C. Chinese astronomers record the sighting of a solar eclipse.

1360 B.C. Chinese mathematicians introduce a nonpositional number system (with no zero). It was multiplicative (e.g., 300 was written as 3 together with the symbol for 100) and additive (1,975 was written as 1,000 + 900 + 70 + 5).

Technology

1200 B.C. Offshore fisherman in Peru use rafts and boats (cabalitos) made from reeds.

1200 B.C. From this time Olmec sculptors in Mesoamerica carve human–animal figurines and giant human heads at sites at La Venta and San Lorenzo near the Gulf coast. Many are ritually destroyed in 900 B.C.

1200 B.C. The Egyptians connect the Nile River to the Red Sea with a canal at Lake Timsah.

1150 B.C. Chinese workmen cast bells in bronze.

1150 B.C. Craftsmen in Cyprus and Mycenae (in Greece) decorate objects with vitreous enamel (colored glass).

1100 B.C. Chinese craftsmen introduce spinning to produce yarn from wool and cotton.

1050 B.C. Dorian invaders from Anatolia introduce ironworking into Greece.

1000 B.C. Farmers in Egypt and Mesopotamia fertilize their crops using animal dung.

1000 B.C. Chinese scribes write using brushes and black ink made from soot and a solution of gum. The writing surface used is bamboo strips or paper made from tree bark.

1000 B.C. The kite is invented in China, arguably the first heavier-than-air flying object.

980 B.C. Chinese writer Lu Tsan-ning recommends using steam to sterilize objects (not necessarily for medical purposes).

950 B.C. The Phoenicians make Tyrian purple dye from the *Murex* sea mollusk. It is so rare and expensive that only kings and emperors have clothes dyed with it.

900 B.C. Chinese people use cast metal coins in the shape of shovels or knives.

850 B.C. The Chinese use natural gas for lighting, conveying it along bamboo "pipes." The gas is probably methane (natural gas) from underground deposits of petroleum.

Science

1350 B.C. Chinese farmers are growing more than one crop in the same year on the same land.

1350 B.C. An Egyptian text describes the symptoms of leprosy.

1200 B.C. Astronomers in Babylon construct an instrument for determining when a star is due south of their observatory.

1000 B.C. People in Siberia in northern Russia keep herds of domestic reindeer.

1000 B.C. The Hindu calendar of 360 days (12 lunar months of 27 or 28 days) is introduced in India.

1000 B.C. The Phoenicians of the Mediterranean develop a 22-letter alphabet.

1000 B.C. Etruscan craftsmen in northern Italy make false teeth from gold, probably more for show than for function.

975 B.C. The Hebrews introduce the Gezer lunar calendar (with 12 months of 27 or 28 days).

950 B.C. Farmers in northern and central Europe cultivate oats, a cereal crop better suited than wheat to the wetter, cooler climate of the region. It was soon grown in northern Britain and is still associated with Scotland, where people make it into porridge.

900 B.C. Farmers in Mesopotamia (present-day Iraq) use irrigation systems to improve the yields of their crops.

763 B.C. Babylonian astronomers observe and record an eclipse of the Sun. About 30 years later Chinese astronomers do the same.

850 B.C. Smyrna (now Izmir, Turkey) becomes the site of the first known arch bridge (built of stone).

800 B.C. Egyptians use artificially heated incubators to hatch eggs.

700 B.C. Phoenician sailors use biremes (boats with two rows of oars). Later, Greek boatbuilders add a pointed ram at the waterline at the front of the vessel to make it a more effective warship.

691 B.C. Assyrian King Sennacherib (reigned 705–681 B.C.) builds an aqueduct to carry water 50 miles (80 km) from a tributary of the Greater Zab River to supply his capital city Nineveh (present-day Mosul) with water.

600 B.C. Greek artist and metalworker Glaucus of Chios (fl. 5th century B.C.) produces an alloy that melts easily and uses it to solder metals.

530 B.C. Greek engineer Eupalinus of Megara (fl. 6th century B.C.) builds a 3,600-foot (1,100-m) tunnel through a mountain on Samos to carry water across the island.

515 B.C. Ionian philosopher Anaximander of Miletus (c.611–c.547 B.C.) introduces the sundial to Greece as a means of telling the time.

513 B.C. Persian King Darius (c.558–c.486 B.C.) builds a 2,000-foot (600-m) pontoon bridge to carry his invading army across the Bosporus (near present-day Istanbul).

424 B.C. In the war between Athens and Sparta (in Greece), the attackers of Delion use a flamethrower consisting of a tube containing burning charcoal, sulfur, and tar, mounted on a wheeled carriage and using bellows to blow the flames forward.

Technology

---

750 B.C. Greek poet Homer refers to the process of burning sulfur to fumigate plants and thereby kill pests.

600 B.C. Mayan people of Central America make a chocolate drink using pods of the cacao plant.

550 B.C. Greek mathematician and philosopher Pythagoras (c.580–c.500 B.C.) determines the relationship between the length of a vibrating string and the pitch of the note it produces.

434 B.C. Ionian philosopher Anaxagoras (c.500–c.428 B.C.) postulates that the Sun is a ball of hot rock.

430 B.C. Greek mathematician and philosopher Zeno of Elea (c.490–c.430 B.C.) expresses four mathematical paradoxes in order to challenge the notions of space and time generally accepted in his day.

400 B.C. At about this time Greek physician Hippocrates of Kos (c.460–c.377 B.C.), traditionally thought to be the originator of the doctor's Hippocratic oath, describes human anatomy and various diseases. He relates some of them to the environment, thus recognizing that some disorders may have natural causes.

400 B.C. Chinese people use a counting board for calculations and record keeping.

400 B.C. Mayan mathematicians use a place-value number system, to base 20, that includes a symbol for zero.

Science

Timelines 400 B.C.–0 A.D.

Technology

350 B.C. According to Greek philosopher Theophrastus of Eresus (*c*.372–*c*.287 B.C.) metalworkers in Greece and Italy begin using coal as a fuel.

283 B.C. Greek engineers build the 380-foot (115-m) Pharos lighthouse at Alexandria (Egypt), one of the Seven Wonders of the Ancient World. It is destroyed, probably by an earthquake, in 1375.

250 B.C. Greek scientist and mathematician Archimedes (*c*.287–212 B.C.) invents the screw pump (a coarse screw rotated inside a sloping tube) for raising water for irrigation.

250 B.C. Engineer and scientist Philo of Byzantium (b. *c*.300 B.C.) writes treatises on military and mechanical engineering in which he describes bronze springs for catapults, a chain-and-sprocket drive, gear wheels, and a type of universal joint now called a cardan joint after Italian scientist Jerome Cardan (1501–76), who reinvented it.

250 B.C. Egyptian pharaoh Ptolemy II (309–246 B.C.) rebuilds the canal linking the Nile River to the Red Sea.

230 B.C. Greek inventor Ctesibius of Alexandria (fl. 3rd century B.C.) uses metal leaf springs in his catapults.

220 B.C. Roman political leader Gaius Flaminius (d. 217 B.C.) completes the Via Flaminia, a major road from Rome to the valley of the Po River, soon extended to Rimini.

214 B.C. The main part of the Great Wall of China—a section 1,400 miles (2,250 km) long—is completed.

210 B.C. Egyptian pharaoh Ptolemy IV (*c*.244–203 B.C.) builds a huge 400-foot (120-m) twin-hulled galley that needs 4,000 oarsmen and a crew of 3,250 others. The dry dock (a channel connected to the sea that can later be flooded) is invented to build it.

Science

387 B.C. In Athens Greek philosopher Plato (*c*.428–*c*.348 B.C.) opens an academy for the pursuit of philosophical and scientific teaching and research.

350 B.C. Greek scientist and philosopher Aristotle (384–322 B.C.) includes the biological sciences in his basic philosophy. He forms a classification scheme for animals and plants.

330 B.C. Greek scientist and philosopher Aristotle (384–322 B.C.) proposes that the Earth is at the center of the Universe and that the Sun, Moon, planets, and stars orbit around it.

300 B.C. Greek mathematician Euclid (fl. 300 B.C.) produces *Elements*, a book of geometry theorems.

300 B.C. Greek philosopher Theophrastus of Eresus (*c*.372–*c*.287 B.C.) produces a detailed study of 550 species of plants. Five years later he publishes *De Lapidibus* (On Stones), in which he describes 70 minerals.

240 B.C. Chinese astronomers make the first records of what becomes known as Halley's comet.

235 B.C. Greek mathematician Eratosthenes of Cyrene (*c*.276–*c*.194 B.C.) calculates the circumference of the Earth. Ten years later he devises the sieve of Eratosthenes as a method of finding prime numbers (numbers that can be divided only by 1 and themselves).

230 B.C. Greek mathematician Apollonius of Perga (*c*.262–*c*.190 B.C.) writes his treatise *Conics*, dealing with conic sections (i.e., the circle, ellipse, parabola, etc.).

200 B.C. Metalworkers in South America use blowpipes to create the draft for furnaces to make alloys of gold and silver.

150 B.C. Greeks and Romans use a screw press for crushing olives to make olive oil.

150 B.C. People in Ireland and Germany make surfaced roads by laying wooden planks across existing tracks.

110 B.C. Roman horsemen begin to use nailed horseshoes.

100 B.C. Roman builders use concrete made from crushed stones and pozzolana (volcanic ash) cement, which sets underwater.

80 B.C. Vertical undershot waterwheels, used for grinding corn, are introduced in eastern Mediterranean countries.

55 B.C. Roman emperor Julius Caesar (100–44 B.C.) orders his troops to build a trestle bridge across the Rhine River, which they complete in ten days.

50 B.C. Chinese seagoing ships use mat-and-batten sails of a type still used on today's junks.

46 B.C. Roman emperor Julius Caesar (100–44 B.C.) introduces the Julian calendar.

30 B.C. Craftsmen in Syria discover the technique of glassblowing, which the Romans soon adopt for making bottles and other objects.

27 B.C. Roman architect Marcus Vitruvius Pollio (b. 70 B.C.) describes gold amalgam, a gold–mercury alloy.

19 B.C. Roman general Marcus Agrippa (63–12 B.C.) organizes the construction of the 13-mile- (21-km-) long Aqua Virgo aqueduct in Rome.

10 B.C. King Herod the Great (c.73–4 B.C.) of Judea builds an open-sea harbor of concrete blocks to serve the new city Caesarea of Palestine (near today's Haifa, Israel).

200 B.C. Astronomers of the Alexandrian school (founded by pharaoh Ptolemy I) develop astronomical instruments, including the astrolabe.

165 B.C. Chinese naked-eye astronomers record the existence of sunspots.

150 B.C. Greek astronomer Hipparchus of Nicaea (c.180–125 B.C.) calculates the distance from the Earth to the Moon and discovers the precession of the equinoxes.

125 B.C. Chinese traveler Chang Ch'ien (c.172–c.114 B.C.) introduces wine grapes into China from the West.

100 B.C. Chinese mathematicians begin to use negative numbers.

75 B.C. Greek physician Asclepiades of Bithynia (c.120–c.30 B.C.) teaches that disease comes from discord in the corpuscles of the body.

55 B.C. Hindu medical system the Ayurveda is developed at about this time and becomes the basis of medical teaching in India for centuries.

52 B.C. Chinese astronomer Ken Shou-Ch'ang makes a form of armillary ring (a metal ring representing the equator, used to observe the stars).

44 B.C. Chinese and Roman astronomers report seeing a red comet; the color is caused by airborne ash from the eruption of Mount Etna in Sicily.

28 B.C. Chinese astronomers begin keeping records of sunspots (and do so until 1638 A.D.).

Glossary

archaeologist A person who finds out how people used to live by uncovering and examining the material remains of past societies.

artifact Any object made by humans.

astrologer A person who studies the positions and aspects of the stars and planets and their supposed effect on events on Earth.

astronomical tables Records of information designed to enable the calculation of planetary positions, lunar phases, eclipses, and information for calendars.

bit Today, a piece of metal held in a horse's mouth attached to reins and used to control a horse while riding; early bits were made of rope or hide.

bronze A hard durable alloy made of copper and tin.

Bronze Age The period of Asian and European prehistory, lasting from about 4000 through 1200 B.C., when most tools were made of bronze.

charcoal A form of carbon made by charring wood in a container, from which air is excluded.

cosmology The study of the origin of the Universe.

curing Preserving meat for future use, and preventing its deterioration.

domestication The adaptation of animals or wild plants through selective breeding to make them useful for humans.

extinct A species of animal or plant that no longer exists.

flint An extremely hard type of black quartz found in sedimentary rocks.

flywheel A heavy wheel that resists changes in speed and helps steady the rotation of a shaft.

herbal medicine A medicine made from plants, such as salicylic acid (aspirin) made from willow bark.

hieroglyphs A system of writing, originating in Egypt and Mexico, which uses pictures to symbolize words.

lapis lazuli A blue semiprecious stone.

lever A simple machine consisting of a rigid bar pivoted on a fixed point and used to transmit force.

lunar Of or relating to the Moon.

Mesoamerica The region comprising

the southern part of Mexico along with the countries of Central America.

Mesolithic A period of the Stone Age between the Paleolithic and the Neolithic, from about 8000 through 27000 B.C.

meteorite A rock fragment that is of extraterrestrial origin.

Neolithic The period of Asian and European prehistory between 9000 and 2000 B.C., when crops and animals were domesticated and early farming societies developed.

new Moon The first visible crescent of the Moon.

Paleolithic An ancient period of development, beginning about 2.5 million years ago, in which humans used basic chipped stone tools.

papyrus A writing material used by the ancient Egyptians, made by beating together the stems of certain reeds.

pastoralists People who primarily live by raising and herding livestock, such as cattle, sheep, and goats.

Phoenicians A maritime trading culture that spread across the Mediterranean from modern-day

Lebanon during the period 1550 B.C. through 300 B.C.

placenta A membranous vascular organ that develops in female mammals during pregnancy through which the embryo is nourished.

planetarium An apparatus or display representing the celestial bodies and other astronomical phenomena, and the building or room containing this apparatus.

pyramid Any huge structure with a square base and four sloping, triangular sides meeting at the top.

rock carving The depiction of animals, figures, and abstract design on a rock surface.

solar eclipse When the Moon blocks all or part of the Sun's light from reaching the Earth's surface, because the Moon passes directly between the Earth and the Sun.

Sumerians People who lived in the south of Mesopotamia as far south as the Persian Gulf.

ziggurat A temple of rectangular tiers (large at the base and small at the top), built with a core of unfired mud bricks and an outer covering of fired bricks.

Index

Words and page numbers in **bold** type indicate main references to the various topics. Page numbers in *italic* refer to illustrations. An asterisk (*) before a page range indicates mentions on each page rather than unbroken discussion.

A

Acheulian industry 9
acupuncture 36, *36*, 99
agriculture and farming 30–3, *94–102
see also* cereals
Agrippa, Marcus 83, 105
Akkadian civilization 67
alcohol 96, 101
alloys 49
alphabets 27, *29*, 100, 102
Anaximander of Miletus 103
animals
    classification 104
    domestication 22–5, *22-3*
    extinct/endangered 25
    see also individual animals

Apollonius of Perga 104
aqueducts 103
    Roman 82–3, 105
arches *82–3*, 83, 96, 98, 103
Archimedes 67, **72–5**, 104
    Archimedes' Principle 75
    mathematics 75
    weapons 74, 90
Aristotle 69, 104
arithmetic books 28–9
arrowheads 95
artillery
    ancient 88–93
    Greek 88–9, *89*–90, 91, *91*
    Roman *88*, 89, *89*, 90
Asclepiades of Bithynia 105
Asclepius (Aesculapius) 37
    pillar from temple to *37*
astrologers 101
astronomy *99–105
    comets 105
    instruments 105
    Mayan 85–6
    sunspots 105
Aurignacian Industry 9
automata 68
axes 9, 94
axles 18–19, 68, 71, 97
Ayurvedic medicine 37, 105

B

Babbage, Charles 70
ballista *88*, 89, *89*
barges *43*, 101
battering rams 91, *91*, 100
beam balances 96
beam press 101
beer 95, 101
bellows 100
bells 102
biological sciences, classification scheme 104
bitumen 99
blades 9–10, 95, 100
blowpipes 105
boats 11, **42–5**, 95, 97
    anchors 98
    barges *43*, 101
    biremes 103
    canoes 42, 96
    coracles 42, *42*
    dugout 42
    galleys 104
    reed boats 96, 101
    sail development 42–5, 97, 105
    triremes *44–5*
Book of the Dead *32*
boomerangs 94
bridges 103, 105
bronze 48, 97, 99, 100, 102

C

Caccus, Appius Claudius 80
calendars 50–3
  Babylonian 53
  Chinese 53, 98
  Egyptian 50–1, 97
  Hebrew 102
  Hindu 53, 102
  Julian 105
  Mayan *53*, 84, 86–7, *87*
  Sumerian 52–3, 98
camels, domestication 24, 98
cams 71
canals 102, 104
canoes 42, 96
cardan joints 104
catapults 88–90, 92–3, 103, 104
cats, domestication 25, 97, 99
cattle, domestication 23, 24, 95
cereals 94, 95, 96, 101, 102
  origins of 14–17, *14-15*
  see also agriculture and farming
Chandragupta Maurya 76–7
Chang Ch'ien 105
chariots 19–20, *20*, 100
chickens, domestication 23, 96

China, Great Wall 104
chocolate 103
choppers 7–8
clay
  models 94
  pottery 33, 95, 98
  tablets *27*
  water pipes 99
clocks 97
  water clocks 69, 101
clothes 10
cloth making 11, 96
coal 104
coins 102
concrete 105
copper 48, 49, 96, 97, 100
coracles 42, *42*
cotton 97, 98
counting boards 103
cranks 71
Cro-Magnon people 9–10, 95
Ctesibius of Alexandria 69, 104
Cuicuilco 62, 64
cultivation 16–17
cuneiform writing 26–7, *27*, 28, 98
  numbers 28
Cup of Nestor 46

D

dams 97, 101
Darius, King of Persia 103

Delphi oracle 58, *59*
Dionysius the Elder of Syracuse 88
distaffs 96
distillation 96, 101
dogs, domestication 25, 94
donkeys, domestication 97
Dresden Codex 85
drills 100
dry docks 104
dye 102

E

Ebers Papyrus 101
elephants, domestication 99
Eratosthenes of Cyrene 104
Euclid 104
Eupalinus of Megara 103

F

farming *see* agriculture and farming; cereals
Fertile Crescent 16, 17, *30–1*, 96
files (metal) 100
fire making 12–13, *13*, 94
fire-raisers 91, *91*
fishing 11, 94, 95
flamethrowers 93, 103

Flaminius, Gaius 104
flint 9
flywheels 20–1
food preservation 32–3
fumigation 103

G

galleys (boats) 104
Ganga River technology 76–9
gas 102
gears 68–70, *68*
geese, domestication 99
glass 98, 102
glassblowing 105
Glaucus of Chios 103
goats, domestication 23, 24, 94
gold 46–8, 99
    amalgam 105
    for false teeth 102
grapes 97, 105
Greece, temples and tombs 58–61
grindstones 33
Guinea pigs, domestication 24, 100

H

Halley's comet 104
hammers 9, 94
    water-powered 70
harbors 105

harpoons 95
Harrison, John 70
helmets *48*
Hera, Temple of 59–60
Hero of Alexandria 68, 71
Herod the Great 105
hieroglyphics 26, 97
Hipparchus of Nicaea 105
Hippocrates 103
Homo erectus 8–9, 12, 94
Homo habilis 7–8, 94
Homo sapiens 9, 94
horses 24, 97
horseshoes 105
house construction 95, 96
humans, early 6–11, *8*

I

Imhotep 36
iron 48–9, 100, 101, 102
irrigation 77–8, 102
Ishango bone 50

J

jungle fowl, domestication 96

K

Ken Shou-Ch'ang 105
kites 102

knives 94

L

lamps 94
Lebombo bone 50
leprosy 102
levers 66, 68, 72
llamas, domestication 98
locks (for doors) 97

M

machines 66–71
mammoths, woolly 94
maps 99, 100
marble sculptures 97
mathematics 100, 103
    arithmetic books 28–9
    conic sections 104
    geometry 104
    see also numbers
Mayan civilization 84–7, 103
    astronomy 85–6
    calendar *53*, 84, 86–7, *87*
    numbers 86, 103
    pyramids 63–4, *63*
    writing 84
medicine 100, 101
    ancient 34–7
    Ayurvedic 37, 105
    Babylonian 34
    Chinese *35*, 36
    Hindu 105

metals, use of 46–9
metalworking 104
    in India 79, *79*
minerals 104
Minoan civilization 58
mirrors 93, 96, 100

N

Neanderthal people 9
Nile floods 97
numbers 28–9
    Babylonian 100
    Chinese 101
    cuneiform 28
    Egyptian 29, 97
    Mayan 86, 103
    negative 105
    prime 104
    see also mathematics

O

obsidian 96
Olduwan Industry 8
Olmec civilization 62–3,
    101, 102

P

papyrus 27, *32–3*, 98
parasols 99
Parthenon 60, *61*
perfume 100
Périgordian Industry 9
Pharos Lighthouse 104
Philo of Byzantium 104

pigs, domestication 23,
    95
plants
    classification 104
    fumigation 103
Plato 104
plows *32*, 66, *67*, 97, 100
plowshares 100
Pont du Gard *82–3*, 83
potter's wheels *19*, 69
pottery 33, 95, 98
Ptolemy II, Pharaoh 104
Ptolemy IV, Pharaoh 104
pyramids
    construction 38–41,
        39, 41
    Great Pyramid of
        King Khufu 99
    **Mesoamerican
        62–5**, *63*
    pyramid of Djoser
        38, 98
    Red Pyramid, Dashur
        38–9
Pythagoras 103

Q

quartz 9

R

rebus writing 84
record keeping 28, 95
reed boats 96, 101
reindeer, domestication
    102

Rhind Papyrus 100
rice 16, 76–7, *76–7*, 95
roads 105
    Roman 80-3, *80, 81*,
        104
rock shelters 98

S

saws 96
screw presses 105
screw pumps 68, 73, *74*,
    104
seed drills 101
Sennacherib, King of
    Assyria 103
shadoofs *66*, 67, 100
sheep, domestication
    23, 24, 94
siege ladders 91, *91*
silk 11, 98
silver 46
sleds 95
slingshots *90*, 92–3
snowshoes 99
soap 98
Solutrean Industry 10
spears 94
spinning 96, 102
spinning wheels 21
steel 49, 78
stelae 60, *60*, 84
sterilization, by steam
    102
Stonehenge 97, 100,
    101